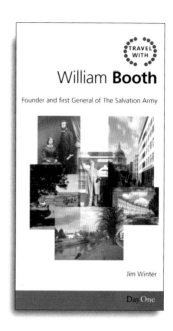

TRAVEL WITH

William **Booth**

Founder and first General of The Salvation Army

Jim Winter

Day One

Series Editor: Brian H Edwards

Day One

TRAVEL WITH
William **Booth**

51

④ The love of his life

Good Friday 1852 was a momentous day for William Booth. It marked his entrance into full-time Christian service, and it was also the day on which he fell in love with Catherine—who later became the 'Mother' of The Salvation Army. Booth was sent to work in Spalding, Lincolnshire, and refined the methods of evangelism that he first began among the poor in Nottingham

Catherine Mumford was born in Ashbourne, Derby, on 17 January 1829, the only daughter of five children. Her father, a coachbuilder, moved the family to Boston in Lincolnshire when she was five years old. From Boston they moved to Russell Street in what was then the leafy South London suburb of Brixton. Catherine was a serious child and deeply interested in spiritual matters. She is reputed to have read the Bible through eight times by the time she was twelve! Catherine was not a healthy child and never a healthy woman—although she bore seven children during her thirty-five year marriage to William. At the age of fourteen she developed curvature of the spine and incipient tuberculosis. Prolonged bouts of illness left her weak, but gave her time to read and think. She developed strong opinions on a number of issues including the use of alcohol, animal welfare, and women's rights.

Throughout her life Catherine was a strict teetotaller, and was prominent in the temperance movement. It is quite possible that

Above: Catherine Mumford pictured in her early twenties

Facing page: Picturesque Lincolnshire; the Booths made Spalding their home, establishing a fruitful ministry

---

77

⑥ 'I have found my destiny!'

On an East London street, William Booth discovered the work that was to consume the rest of his life. As founder and head of the Christian Mission—later to become the Salvation Army—he reached out to the destitute and desperate in one of the poorest areas of the capital. The Mission rapidly expanded as others joined him

In February 1865 the Booths moved to London. They were by now in their mid-thirties with six children. With William's support, Catherine accepted an invitation to preach at a mission in Rotherhithe, in London's docklands on the south bank of the Thames. Her reputation had also reached the more affluent chapels in the West End of the capital. William was conducting a campaign in Lincolnshire and although he did not feel a deep sense of call to the capital, he agreed that it would be best for the whole family to move down from Leeds and make their base in London. They rented 31 Shaftesbury Road, a large family house in Hammersmith, West London. William headed back to Yorkshire to take a short mission in the cathedral city of Ripon. Every day, until the late spring, Catherine would make the long, exhausting, journey across the River Thames, to the rough and dangerous dockland areas, often returning home well after midnight.

Meanwhile, William had returned to London with the idea

Above: The Blind Beggar in Whitechapel. It was near this building William Booth stopped on a July evening, and preached the gospel

Facing page: The City of London. During 1865, Catherine Booth preached at a mission at Rotherhithe in the docklands

CONTENTS

© Day One Publications 2003 First printed 2003

All Scripture quotations are taken from the Authorized Version

A Catalogue record is held at The British Library   ISBN 1 903087 35

Published by Day One Publications 3 Epsom Business Park, Kiln Lane, Epsom, Surrey KT17 1JF

☎ 01372 728 300 FAX 01372 722 400 email—sales@dayone.co.uk www.dayone.co.uk   All rights reserved

Design: Steve Devane   Printed by Alderson Brothers, Molesey, Surrey

North America, Africa, India and Ceylon. South America was the only continent not to see him.

In his homeland his travels were equally remarkable, including a total of seven pioneering motorcade campaigns, the first in 1904 when the automobile was still an exciting and, to many, a dangerous modern contraption.

But it is the spiritual journeyings of the man that should most challenge and thrill us. His vision was so intense and his faith so strong that he never doubted what God could do with illiterate, gin-soaked roughs in a Whitechapel pub—that they could be saints; he never doubted what God could make of homeless, workless, dispirited men huddled on a London bridge —that they could be Kingdom-builders. And so it was! Around the world, it was men like these, and their dissolute, downtrodden women, who became The Salvation Army.

I trust that as you follow in the footsteps of this great servant of Christ you will also catch something of his passion, and take one more step—or maybe your first—along the road of faith. God be with you as you go!

General John Larsson
International Leader of
The Salvation Army

William Booth, the Founder of The Salvation Army, was a great traveller. His first journey, enforced by unemployment and poverty, was from his native Nottingham to London. His last, some 63 years later, was the five-mile triumphant progress of his funeral cortege through the streets of that city, now lined with thousands of the rich and the poor to honour him for his faith and his compassion.

Between these two, William Booth travelled further and more widely throughout the world than any other Christian evangelist up to that time. Journeys to Japan and the Far East, three times to Australia and New Zealand, often to the continent and Scandinavia, to

" About my Fathers business."

William Booth

Aug 5 07.

Meet William Booth

'While women weep, as they do now, I'll fight; while children go hungry, as they do now, I'll fight; while men go to prison, in and out, in and out, as they do now, I'll fight; while there is a drunkard left, while there is a poor lost girl on the streets, while there remains one dark soul without the light of God, I'll fight—I'll fight to the very end!'

These words, spoken by the frail, sick, almost blind, eighty-year-old, nearly a century ago, still echo round the world. In the streets of major cities and in remote places on every continent, Salvation Army officers continue the work of bringing 'soup, soap and salvation' to the poor and needy. The sight of the uniform and the sound of the brass band still bring hope to millions of the world's poor and lost.

As a young man William Booth saw the poverty and suffering that surrounded him in the streets of Nottingham and the East End of London, but he could not have imagined that the organisation he founded would have such a world-wide impact. Nearly a hundred years after his death, the Salvation Army works in over 100 countries, with 14000 Corps using more than 140 languages. It operates over two thousand food distribution centres, and its hospitals care for twenty-seven million patients annually. Each year over forty thousand people are given accommodation in hostels and residential centres and more than ten thousand missing relatives are traced by the Missing Person's Bureau. Coupled to this is the work among refugees, alcoholics, drug addicts, prostitutes, offenders and those contemplating suicide.

Driven by a love for Christ and the souls of men, this remarkable man launched a campaign against the sin that brought misery to millions. At first reviled, later honoured, his is the story of what God can do with a life entirely devoted to Jesus Christ.

Left: *General Booth on Motor tour in 1907*

① Riot!

Violence broke out on the streets of an English seaside resort as a mob ferociously attacked a young woman Salvation Army captain and her small company. Along the coast, another woman was kicked to death. This was just the beginning of widespread opposition as the newly formed Salvation Army, founded by William Booth, waged war on sin and poverty in cities and towns throughout Britain

Above: William Booth in his late twenties

Facing page: Sea front, Worthing

From the steps of Worthing Town Hall, Lt Col. Thomas Wisden looked out across the crowded streets. It was 11.20 pm on a sultry summer night, but the combination of the gaslights and the moonlight enabled him to pick out the white skull and crossbones on the dark banners waved by the angry mob that assembled before him. The officer was facing the self-styled 'Skeleton Army'. As presiding magistrate, Wisden set about the task that lay before him. He nervously fingered the paper in his hand. It was Wednesday 20 August 1884.

The events of the previous weekend had now reached their climax. Wisden drew courage from the sight of the red tunics of forty mounted Royal Dragoons, who formed a barrier between himself and the seething mass of people bent on havoc. Drafted in from the Preston Barracks at nearby Brighton to halt the sickening violence and destruction that had engulfed the town over the previous few days, they formed his only real protection. The local

police had lost control and this had contributed to the mayhem that engulfed the streets. Those who were still on duty were exhausted. The prospect of anarchy was both real and immediate.

Thomas Wisden began to address the crowd, his words almost lost in the night air as the Skeletons sang, *Rule Britannia* in open defiance. Their voices reached a great crescendo as they came to the words, 'Britons NEVER, NEVER, NEVER shall be slaves'! Wisden remained resolute as he read, 'Our Sovereign Lady the Queen chargeth and commandeth all persons being assembled immediately to disperse themselves and peaceably to depart to their habitations or their lawful business, upon the pains contained in the act … God save the Queen.' This was the Riot Act, introduced in 1715 as the final sanction of the State against riotous assembly. A hail of bricks met Wisden's words. It would be almost two hours before the police and Dragoons could disperse the fighting mob. Worthing had become a battlefield.

In the days to come there would be many allegations of police brutality. An innocent bystander—a pastry cook named Semadini—died from multiple head injuries, said to have been inflicted by police truncheons; and a thirteen year old boy—Frederick Thompson—was reported to have been 'beaten in a savage manner' by local constables. This was the

Left: Worthing Town Hall. The original building, demolished in 1968, stood on the corner of South Street and Warwick Street

Facing page: 'riotous proceedings at Worthing'—as portrayed by an artist at the time

climax of a war that had been declared on the town the previous April, by another army—absent from the evening's affairs—and with an objective far different from those who had assembled at the Town Hall.

'Some of my best men are women'

The summer of 1884 held great prospect for the businessmen and hoteliers of Worthing. Throughout the season excursion trains brought holidaymakers and Sunday day-trippers into the English South Coast seaside town. During the first half of the eighteenth century the town had risen from social obscurity to respectability. Worthing was a fashionable place for the middle-class Victorian to bring his family now that the railway had put it within easy reach of London. That very summer the playwright, Oscar Wilde, was in residence at Esplanade House, working on one of his most popular plays: *The Importance of Being Earnest*—surnaming one of its main characters, Mr Worthing.

In April 1884, Ada Smith, a twenty three year old Captain in a very different Army, had arrived to take command of the local Corps. Founded by William Booth in 1865 as the East London Christian Mission, the Salvation Army (as it became known from 1878) had already made its mark upon many of the cities and towns across the country. Booth and his followers, shocked by the poverty and vice

Above: Early Salvationists in Worthing. The make up of many bands varied widely with old brass instruments, drums, cymbals, banjos

Facing page: Salvation Army Citadel, Crescent Road, Worthing

that had engulfed the underclass in Victorian Britain, were determined to wage war against the moral and social evils of the day. Marching under the banner of 'Blood and Fire', the Salvationists sought the people that the churches of the day had largely ignored. This kind of religion was not to be found in comfortable pews, but on the streets and in the hovels where so many of the population lived. Booth had said, 'Some of my best men are women.' Ada Smith was one of his best men!

The Worthing Salvation Army Corps had been founded in 1883. Setting up their barracks in the aptly named Prospect Place, they began their meetings in a rented hall in Montague Street, which ran parallel to the seafront. Regular street processions were a marked feature of the Army's strategy. Targeting the poorer parts of town, particularly the public houses and places of bawdy entertainment, they set about 'converting' the local populace. Opposition was immediate. The town's publicans feared for their loss of trade, and the Army's provocative language and military terminology angered many local dignitaries.

During the following year, at the height of the disturbances, Ada Smith wrote, 'So with loaded guns and Holy Ghost ammunition, we are in the field, and with all our might we are pouring red-hot bullets of Calvary death, judgement, heaven, and hell into the ears and hearts of the vast crowds of people, and by the power of God it is taking mighty effects.' Such language confused, disturbed, and even frightened, those whose only acquaintance with religion was the formality of the established churches. The Salvationists had a mixed reception from the local clergy. One invited them to a communion service, whilst another wrote, 'The Salvation Army stinketh in my nostrils.' The churches, however, were united in their dislike of the Army's tactics in the town.

It was feared that the Sunday parades through the town would have a detrimental effect upon the trade brought in by the summer's day-trippers. The fiercest opposition came from one of the local newspapers, the newly founded *Worthing Gazette*, which 'doubted whether such disgraceful scenes on the Sabbath had ever been witnessed before.' Skirmishes followed between the Army and some of the rougher elements of the local population. As a result, the officer in charge, Frances Kirkby had decided to suspend the street parades.

With the arrival of Captain Ada Smith such timidity was swept aside. Confrontation was inevitable. Her motto was, 'If the devil doesn't attack us, we must attack him!' With great determination Ada led her troops into battle. They numbered only about twenty, but this did not daunt their young captain. Armed with the conviction that they were marching on the side of truth and righteousness, they made their way from the meeting place in Montague Street into the

traditional working class areas of town. Firstly to the nearby fishermen's quarters at Prospect Place and New Street, moving on to Clifton Road, where the labourers and workmen lived. The people of Clifton Road were a close knit, self-sufficient community. The two rows of terraced houses have since been demolished, but the public house, the *Jolly Brewers* still stands. The residents particularly resented the Salvation Army's attempts to 'save' them, and it was from here that the most persistent and prolonged opposition would come. The moment Ada's little army left Montague Street and turned towards the seafront, they

Above: Formerly the Jolly Brewer, Clifton Road, the focal point of opposition to The Salvation Army

were met by a fusillade of rotten vegetables and eggshells filled with paint. Soon the missiles would be harder and the injuries more serious.

The Skeleton Army

As the persecution intensified, William Booth ordered Ada Smith to cease the parades until he obtained written assurance of their safety from the Chief Constable of Sussex. Receiving no satisfaction by July, he sent a memorandum to the Home Secretary, followed three days later by a telegram. By the beginning of August, with the Home Office still dithering and Booth cautious, Ada Smith took the matter into her own hands and ordered her troops back on to the streets. On Sunday 17 August 1884 Worthing echoed once more with the sound of the Salvationists' songs.

By now the opposition was well supported and better organised. The 'Worthing Excelsior Skeleton Army' was one of many such 'armies' scattered around the country in direct opposition to Booth's organisation. Two years previous to the Worthing riots reports flooded in from many parts of the country citing over six hundred instances of assault on the Salvation Army's members. The ammunition ranged from rotten vegetables, dead rats and cats, to rocks. In some cases Booth's soldiers were 'fire bombed' with burning coals and sulphur. It was not unusual for chamber pots to be emptied from the windows of buildings as Salvationists paraded by. Serious injury and even death followed many of the savage beatings

Above: From the Illustrated London News, August 1884, drawings of the Worthing riots showing the old Town Hall and George Head's shop

endured by Booth's troops. In Hastings, the first Salvationist martyr, Susannah Beattie was felled by a hail of rocks and kicked to death as she lay helpless on the ground. Fatalities were also reported at Guildford and Shoreham.

The Skeletons had little difficulty in recruitment to their cause. They were largely made up of anarchic social misfits, who, in other circumstances, would probably be fighting each other. Like so many that have engaged in riots and destruction before and since, all they needed was a common cause and an excuse to wreak their havoc. Encouraged and funded by a strange alliance of brewers, publicans, pimps and local civic leaders, the Skeletons had found their cause—the destruction of The Salvation

Army. Some local town councillors even put pressure on the police to turn a blind eye to the Skeletons' activities. In some ways, the Skeletons aped Booth's methods. As well as the skull and crossbones, one banner read, 'beef, beer and bacca', in response to the Salvationists' 'soup, soap and salvation.'

Trouble was inevitable and on Sunday 17 August it arrived! Police lined the streets as Booth's troops marched, preceded by a large group of chanting Skeletons. By the time they had reached Bath Place violence erupted. Amid a hail of bricks and bottles, Ada Smith and her soldiers clawed their way back to the relative safety of their meeting hall in Montague Street. Even brave Ada Smith thought it wise to cancel the evening meeting.

'We'll jump on old Head!'

On Monday evening, as the Salvationists met for worship, the faint sound of chanting could be heard above the prayers and Bible readings. The volume slowly increased, until suddenly the building shook as rocks and other heavy missiles rained upon it. The high windows shattered and the assembled company dived for cover as stones and broken glass poured down upon them. The police quickly moved in and arrests were made; one of them being William Medhurst, a prominent Skeleton leader. Medhurst's arrest brought some respite for the beleaguered Salvationists, as the angry crowd now turned their attention to the police. On arriving at the police station in Ann Street they demanded the release of their leader. The police had barricaded themselves in and neither Medhurst nor any of the constables were going to leave that night! The building was under siege. This did not last long, however, for the crowd had one last port of call before their ammunition and energy were spent.

George Head's ironmonger's shop was in Montague Street. A quiet, bearded man, Head was a trustee of the Montague Hall. He had resolutely insisted, despite strong and violent opposition from many in the town, that the Army could hold their meetings there. Head was, at that time, the most hated man in Worthing. This would be the second time in a matter of days in which violence would be directed towards him and his shop. Later in the year, the mob would gather again to attempt to burn down his premises.

George Head never became a

Opposite page: The General makes a return to Worthing in August 1907

Left: Montague Street, which runs parallel to the seafront. The Worthing Salvationists, founded in 1883, began their meetings in a rented hall here

Salvationist so why then, did he bravely support Booth's activities in Worthing? Like Booth, he hated alcohol. His father, John, had been an alcoholic and had persistently beaten his mother. In 1863, Head came home to witness such a beating, and in trying to protect her, he himself had been injured by his father; the police were called and John Head was arrested. George loved his father but hated the drink that had wrecked his home and family. William Booth, Ada Smith and George Head had a common enemy.

The shop's windows soon shattered under a fusillade of bricks, the doors buckled under the weight of the heaving mob, and at least ten Skeletons entered the shop. As they set about their mission of carnage, two pistol shots were heard above the sound of the mob. Head was armed! Panic ensued and the Skeletons ran from the shop, two of them bleeding from flesh wounds. The crowd quickly dispersed into the night air. On Wednesday 20 August, Medhurst appeared before the local magistrate receiving a sentence of two month's hard labour for assaulting a policeman. Incensed by this, the Worthing Skeletons launched their all-out assault on the police station. They were determined to rescue their comrade. Sensing that the police were by now unable to control the events that were happening in his town, Lt Col Wisden called for urgent assistance from the army. It was the swift arrival of the Dragoons that prevented the doors of the belcaguered police station from giving way under the heaving mob. With the arrival of the Dragoons

Left: Prospect Place, Worthing, the home of The early Salvation Army

and the reading of the Riot Act, peace was slowly restored to the streets. By one o'clock in the morning of 21 August, the crowd had dispersed. An uneasy calm settled upon the town over the next few days. The Salvation Army continued to march, and the Skeletons continued to oppose them, but there were no major outbreaks of violence. It was not long, however, before the fragile calm was broken!

On Sunday 7 September 1884, as Ada Smith led an afternoon service in Montague Hall, a cacophony of hisses and boos and ribald chants began to erupt from the crowded balcony. The young Salvationist called for order. The chanting intensified. In a desperate attempt to bring the meeting to order, she blew hard upon a whistle. Its shrill sound was picked up by passing policemen, and it was not long before the hall erupted into an appalling scene of violence and destruction, with the assembled worshippers caught up in a melee of fighting police and Skeletons. The building was wrecked and the Skeleton leaders were once more dragged off to the Police Station. This time, pursued by the angry mob, the police securely barricaded themselves in. Returning to the hall, the Skeletons also found the doors barred. There was, however, another target in the same street, and the mob soon turned their attentions to it. They set off, chanting, 'We'll jump on old Head! By and by.'

This time Head was ready for them. As the windows shattered, for the second time in less than three weeks, shots rang out. Edward Olliver, a prominent member of the Excelsiors, fell to the ground. He had been hit in the face and severely wounded. With the sight of Head resolutely standing, revolver in hand, and the fate of their fallen comrade in the balance, the Skeletons fled. Head was arrested and Olliver recovered. Charged with malicious wounding, George Head was acquitted at Maidstone Assizes when he came to trial in early November.

One battle over… the war is just beginning

Eventually, the attacks upon the Worthing corps petered out; Head's shop was targeted again on 5 November 1886, but this time the police were able to prevent serious damage. The last significant attack on the Salvation Army in the town was in February 1888, when a local Skeleton drove his horse and cart through a parade. By this time the Army were settled in their meeting hall—the 'Citadel' in Crescent Road. By now, the attitude of those in local government had changed. There were new members on the town council, more interested in the good name and prosperity of the town than long standing prejudices against William Booth and his organisation. The Salvation Army was given permission to parade through the streets and to preach the gospel in the town. Even shopkeepers in white gloves marshalled their activities. George Head died in 1899 and although he was never

Above: The plaque on Worthing Sea front which commemorates the preaching of the Gospel since 1888

popular, during the last years of his life, many in Worthing paid him a grudging respect.

The battle of Worthing was more or less over—but William Booth's war had barely begun. The events in this town were to be repeated on every continent in the world! Booth was a General who led from the front. During his lifetime he was stoned, punched, and cursed by many. When a fellow officer was spat on as they paraded through an angry mob, Booth remarked, 'Don't wipe it off—it's a medal!' This was the kind of man who inspired Ada Smith and thousands like her to give themselves totally to the cause of Jesus Christ, and with a burning desire to save all men from sin and poverty.

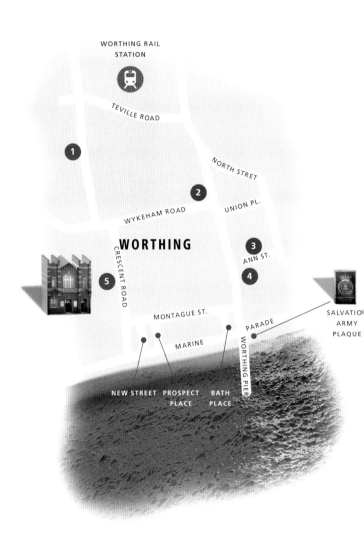

WORTHING RAIL STATION

TEVILLE ROAD

1

NORTH STRET

2

UNION PL.

WYKEHAM ROAD

WORTHING

3

ANN ST.

4

CRESCENT ROAD

5

MONTAGUE ST.

PARADE

SALVATIO ARMY PLAQUE

MARINE

WORTHING PIER

NEW STREET PROSPECT PLACE BATH PLACE

1 *THE JOLLY BREWERS—NOW THE RICHARD COBDEN*
2 TOWN HALL
3 SITE OF POLICE STATION
4 SITE OF OLD TOWN HALL
5 THE SALVATION ARMY CITADEL

TRAVEL INFORMATION

Worthing is situated on the West Sussex Coast 50 miles (80 km) from London. By car—take the A24. There are numerous parking facilities in the town. By rail—Worthing Central Station (from London Victoria—via Gatwick airport). ☎ 08457 4844950 (enquiries). Bus service: ☎ 01903 237 661

There are numerous places of interest in the surrounding area.

Cissbury Ring

Open all year and owned by the National Trust, Cissbury Ring is the second largest hill fort in the country. With views of Beachy Head and the Isle of Wight, the area is also rich in wildlife and was the site of Neolithic flint mining. Address: Off Nepcote Lane, Nr Findon, West Sussex OS Grid Ref:TQ140081

Also in the area: the South Downs; Shoreham Airport and the near-by D-Day Museum; The English Martyrs Catholic Church at Goring has a third-size replica of the famous Sistine Chapel ceiling.

Tourist information: ☎ 01903 210022. email: tourism@worthing.gov.uk

Worthing also offers a mobility scheme for the disabled visitor. Details: ☎ 01903 820 980

Pictured: *Worthing Pier, 1906*

Worthing Pier

The first pier at Worthing dating back to 1862 was designed by Sir Robert Rawlinson and consisted simply of a 960ft (291m) long by 15ft (4.6m) wide promenade deck, with a landing stage. Over the years improvements were made including widening and

lengthening. Disaster struck in 1913 when gale-force winds capsized the pier into the sea. The pier was rebuilt, and over subsequent decades, additions and improvements were made culminating in the structure which can be seen today (pictured above).

Pictured: *Cissbury Ring seen from the air*

2   A silver pencil case

From a comfortable beginning in life, the young William Booth was soon brought face to face with poverty—both in his own family and in the pawnbroker's shop—where he saw the effect of sin on the lives of the poor. A gift from grateful friends convicted him of his own sin and, in the local Methodist Chapel, his life was changed

William Booth was born on 10 April 1829 at 12 Notintone Place, Sneinton, Nottingham. The house still stands, flanked by two adjoining properties in what is now the William Booth Memorial Complex. Opened in 1971, The Salvation Army's Notintone Worship and Community Centre, into which the three houses now nestle, illustrates the work to which William passionately believed God had called him over a century and a half ago. The house itself is a museum to his life and work—the Centre is the living embodiment of his restless struggle to bring the gospel of Jesus Christ to the ordinary people he saw trapped in the endless grind of sin, poverty and social deprivation. Throughout his long life, the 'General', as he came to be known, never laid down his sword. He certainly would have approved the fact that the place bearing his name and marking his entry into this world continues that same fight—the Centre is a place of Christian worship and service. It houses a residential support unit

Facing page and above: Statue of William Booth outside his birthplace at Notintone Place, Nottingham, now the William Booth Memorial Complex

Top: Plaque which commemorates the birth of William Booth

for families at risk, a playgroup, a day-care centre for the elderly, and a club for the disabled and those with learning difficulties. From here the Salvation Army provides food parcels, bedding, clothing and furniture as emergency provision for those in need; as well as a shopping service for disabled and frail elderly people living in the area.

Today, this part of Nottingham is too near the city centre to be called a suburb. In 1829, however, the area was very different. One of William's early biographers described it as: 'A sunny suburb with plenteous flowers and verdant meadows, with the sparkling Trent running through its valleys, and the famed Rudelington Hills rising in the perspective; giving a touch of

Above: The bust of General Booth at the William Booth Birthplace Museum, Notintone Place

rugged beauty to wood, dale and river.' 12 Notintone Place is a six roomed, three storied, building that once stood in a relatively prosperous part of Sneinton.

William's father, Samuel Booth, has been described as a 'speculative builder', whose advice to his son was, 'Make money, and plenty of it'. He had great hopes that William would grow up to be a gentleman. Samuel Booth's own fortune diminished shortly after his second marriage, to William's mother, but he was still relatively prosperous at the time of William's birth and into William's early childhood. In 1824 Samuel married his second wife, Mary Moss, who was thirty-three and the daughter of a Derbyshire farmer. Mary was described as a devoutly Christian woman. William was closer to his mother than to his father whom, in later life, he rarely referred to with any affection. William was the second child of four; his sister Ann having been born in 1827. Emma came in 1831 and Mary in 1833. Within days of his birth, William was baptized at St Stephen's Church, then in the tradition of High Anglicanism.

It would be wrong to assume that in such circumstances, William's early childhood was idyllic; although, on crossing Trent Bridge during one of his motor campaigns as General of the Salvation Army, he did fondly recall happier moments of his childhood: 'My car took me over the Trent, the dear old river along whose banks I used to wander in my boyhood days, sometimes poring over Young's *Night*

Left: St Stephen's Church where William was baptised within days of his birth

Thoughts, reading Henry Kirke White's *Poems*, or, as was frequently the case before my conversion, with a fishing rod in my hand.'

Life among the poor

During William's early years, the city of Nottingham, like other towns and cities, was experiencing rioting and social unrest. Extreme poverty, brought about by a crash in the economy, had hit the city's stocking weaving industry, forcing men into crime and women into prostitution in futile attempts to feed the hunger caused by poverty. All this misery was not lost on William, who in 1890, prefaced his book, *In Darkest England and the Way Out* with a description of the

times: 'When but a mere child, the degradation and helpless misery of the poor stockingers of my native town, wandering gaunt and hunger stricken through the streets, droning out their melancholy ditties, crowding the Union or toiling like galley slaves on relief works for a bare subsistence, kindled in my heart yearnings to help the poor which have continued to this day, and which have had a powerful influence on my whole life.'

Murder and arson were frequent events in the city. During one of the riots, as a mob was making its way to Colnwick Hall, the two year old William may well have witnessed the removal of the railings outside his safe and

comfortable home; they had been
torn down to be used as weapons
by rioters in their frenzied fight
against the army. Colnwick Hall
was razed to the ground in the
conflict.

Shortly after this, the Booth
family moved from Sneinton to
Bleasby, about fifteen miles north
of Nottingham. Samuel Booth's
business steadily improved but, like
so many others of his generation,
he was soon to be plunged into
poverty. William began his
education at the village school. The
business enterprise that drew the
Booths to Bleasby failed, and when
William was six, the family moved
back to Nottingham, this time, to
settle in Bond Street, a short walk
down Sneinton Road towards the
centre of the city. Business began to
pick up again, and Samuel, having
great hopes for his only son and
heir, enrolled him at Samson
Biddulph's Academy. The
Biddulph's had a connection with
the Broad Street Wesleyan
Methodist Chapel, which was to
play an important part in William's
conversion and early ministry.
Samson's son, Samuel, was a
Methodist local preacher.

During this time the people of
Nottingham continued to
experience great hardship and
social unrest. In the severe winter
of 1838 the River Trent froze, and
many of the city's poorest, who
now inhabited the filthy and
crowded streets, died in the arctic
conditions. Starvation was an
imminent threat and troops
stationed in the city were
constantly on the alert for
suspected insurrectionists and
rioters.

The pawnbroker's trade

Samuel Booth was beginning to
experience financial problems that
would eventually end in ruin. At
the age of thirteen William was
withdrawn from Biddulph's
Academy and apprenticed to a
pawnbroker, Francis Eames, in the
poverty ridden Goosegate area of
the city.

This dramatic change in the
family fortunes and William's life
and destiny, was not helped by
what William later recorded as a
rare act of virtue on his father's
part. Samuel had stood surety for
a friend who borrowed a
considerable amount of money.
The man could not pay back the
money and was made bankrupt.
Legally, Samuel was only obliged

Facing page: Biddulph's Academy (now the Lace Market Theatre), this building was where William received much of his education

Left: A city centre Pawnbrokers today. William left Biddulph's at the age of thirteen to start work in Francis Eames' pawnbrokers shop

Below: The original shop door of Francis Eames' pawnbrokers now in the Museum

to redeem the bond that he had made in lieu of the debt, but he felt morally responsible and repaid the whole loan. It is said that this act of chivalry 'provoked the only recorded compliment that his son ever paid him.' In September 1842 Samuel Booth died. The death bed scene had all the trappings of a Christian parting. The family sang the hymn *Rock of ages* as Samuel committed his family to the care of God and died in peace. William's grief was tempered by what he later recorded, 'Deeply though I felt his loss, my grief was all but forbidden by the thought that it was not my mother who had been taken from me.'

Above: The Parish Church St Mary the Virgin, High Pavement, where Samuel Booth married his first wife, Sarah

Opposite: High Pavement, Nottingham

In 1844, an event occurred that shocked everyone, and must have made a deep impression upon the young William Booth. A twenty-nine year old labourer, William Saville, murdered his wife and three children. On conviction, he was sentenced to death by hanging. Public executions were commonplace, but this particular one captured people's imaginations and drew great crowds. Tragedy ensued. A contemporary observer describes the event: 'Eight was the hour of execution, but every available space was occupied long before it arrived. Occasionally there came a cry from the surging masses that someone was fainting or being crushed to death, and if the sufferer were fortunate enough not to be entirely bereft of strength, he or she was lifted up, and permitted to walk to the extremity of the crowd on the shoulders of the people. Saville was led forth, and at three minutes past eight, the drop descended. Almost immediately after, the mighty crowd broke, as it were, in the middle. The anxiety, deep and general, to witness the spectacle, was succeeded by an equally general and still deeper desire to get away from the overpowering and suffocating pressure. The result was positively awful. The greater portion of the house-doors along the pavement were closed, and those who were crushed against the walls by the terrible resistless tide had no means of escape. Twelve persons were killed, and more than a hundred received serious injuries; and of the latter, the deaths of five, after lingering illnesses were clearly traceable to the same catastrophe.'

By now, William was fully engaged in a work that he grew to loathe, but which continued to immerse him in the horrors of poverty. The Goosegate area of Nottingham was one of its poorest and pawnbroking was one of the few thriving industries of the area. There was money to be made out of the poor. His father, who had longed that his son might become a gentleman, had directed William into this particular form of business hoping that, if he could not be a gentleman, at least he had some prospect of becoming rich! Throughout his long life William never spoke directly about the kind of work he was involved in as a youth. He only referred to it as 'trade' or 'business.' However, it would be wrong to conclude that every pawnbroker in the Nottingham of his youth was solely bent on exploiting the poor. The pawnbroker's sign— the three balls—often offered the last vestige of hope for the poor who, for the price of a meal, traded in whatever items of value remained in their homes or adorned their bodies. Sadly, William soon became aware that some of the women who came to him with their Sunday best shawls or even their wedding rings, were doing so to fuel the insatiable thirst of drunken husbands. Many of the pawnbrokers attended nonconformist churches in the area. One, John Knight, became associated with William in the early days of his Christian ministry. Whatever William's distaste for this trade, it was part of God's plan for his life and ministry. Having experienced a degree of poverty in his own family life, he was now plunged into its very depths in Goosegate and brought face to face with its causes and effects.

During the first two years of his apprenticeship William attended St Stephen's Parish Church, where he described the services as 'formal and unfriendly'. It was during this time that he heard the oratory of Feargus O'Connor, a leader of the Chartists—a radical political movement. William's employer Francis Eames was also a supporter.

With the arrival of O'Connor in 1842, the streets of Nottingham once more experienced unrest. His speeches stirred the hearts of the poor and those who saw their poverty as an affront to human dignity. The Chartist supporters clashed with the police and a number of arrests were made. William's heart was stirred by

Above: *Broadway Cinema Complex, formerly Broad Street Methodist Chapel, the site of William's conversion in 1844*

Left: *The Methodist Chapel as it would have been in William's day*

O'Connor's oratory. He became a fervent supporter of the cause, although one suspects that he was more impressed by the man's powerful personality than by his message.

Booth's experiences in this poor part of Nottingham contributed to his life long fight against poverty and its causes. But

John Wesley

Wesley started life at his father's rectory in Epworth, Lincolnshire. His mother, Susannah, had a great spiritual influence on him. At the age of six he was rescued from a fire that had engulfed the house. After his conversion he referred to himself as 'a brand plucked from the burning'. As a fellow of Lincoln College, Oxford he was instrumental in founding the 'Holy Club'. In 1735 he went to America as a missionary but after three years returned home deeply troubled about his soul. On 24 May 1738, at a meeting of Moravian Christians in London, John was converted. Inspired by George Whitefield, Wesley travelled the length and breadth of Britain preaching the gospel. Alongside this he introduced schemes for employment, medical care and education—and established 'class meetings' to support new converts. He was not popular with the established church and was often physically

attacked. It is estimated that Wesley travelled over 250,000 miles and preached 40,000 times during his long ministry.

Above: The statue of John Wesley (1703–1791) outside Wesley's Chapel, City Road, London

even in these early years, he saw the solution as lying beyond the power of the politician. After his death, his son Bramwell said of him: 'My father did not believe that you could make a man clean by washing his shirt.'

The Methodists and William's conversion

During this period, Methodism, not Chartism, became increasingly influential in William's life; particularly the Methodism of the Broad Street Wesleyan Chapel. The chapel, now a cinema, was an imposing building, holding two thousand worshippers. Methodism had grown out of the 'Holy Club', formed by a group of pious Oxford University students, almost a hundred years before William was born. This group of men, which included John and Charles Wesley and George Whitefield, were determined to live lives that were pleasing to God, and later emphasized the necessity for a person to enter into a personal relationship with God through Jesus Christ. Its leading architect was John Wesley.

As William read of this man and his work, his heart was stirred. Here was a kindred spirit—a hero for the young man to follow. In many ways, William's life would follow the pattern of Wesley's. During John Wesley's time the majority of converts were illiterate. His brother, Charles, a gifted poet, set out to teach the new converts the great doctrines

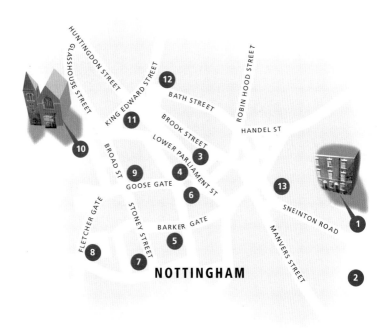

1 WILLIAM BOOTH MEMORIAL COMPLEX
2 ST STEPHEN'S CHURCH
3 SNEINTON HOUSE
4 THE HOUSE IN KID STREET WHERE BOOTH
   FIRST PREACHED
5 SITE OF EAMES PAWNBROKERS
6 HOCKLEY
7 ST. MARY THE VIRGIN CHURCH
8 BIDDULPH'S ACADEMY
9 THE WESLEY CHAPEL (NOW CINEMA)
10 THE WESLEY CENTRE
11 WILLIAM BOOTH MEMORIAL HALL
12 BENDIGO'S TOMB
13 SITE OF BOOTH'S THIRD HOME IN BOND ST

of the Bible through the singing of stirring hymns. It was the singing of the early Methodists that attracted so many to their meetings. This was an attraction for William also, and something that influenced him greatly when he too became a nationally known evangelist.

William was at a crossroads in his life. He was unhappy and although he was not a bad young man, he was conscious that all was not well with his soul—he was a sinner. One of the preachers at the Broad Street Wesleyan Chapel was Isaac Marsden, and it was Marsden's preaching that contributed to this condition and pointed him to its solution. It is

difficult to tell how much Marsden influenced young William, but it is clear that God used this man to bring William to a point where he knew that he must do something about the state of his soul. William's conversion was not as dramatic as many would experience later under his own ministry. He had received a silver pencil case as a mark of gratitude from two friends to whom he had done a favour. In fact, it was no favour at all. William had profited from the transaction and had kept that fact from them! His conscience troubled him and he realized that here was the barrier that separated him from a living relationship with God, and denied him peace of heart and mind. Like the rich young ruler who came to Jesus and was told, 'This one thing you lack', William felt the conviction that here was the one thing that he possessed that must be given back with an open confession of his sin. Later in life he said that he could recall nothing of the speeches of Feargus O'Connor that had stirred him so much, nor any of the sermons that he heard in those early days at Broad Street Chapel, but he recalled vividly the events leading up to the great change that was to shape the rest of his life: 'I remember, as if it were yesterday, the spot in the corner of the room under the chapel, the hour, the resolution to end the matter, the rising up and rushing forth, the finding of the young fellow I had chiefly wronged, the acknowledgement of my sin, the return of the pencil-case, the instant rolling away from my heart of the guilty burden, the peace that came in its place, and the going forth to serve my God and my generation from that hour. It was in the open street that this great change passed over me, and if I only could have possessed the flagstone on which I stood at that happy moment, the sight of it occasionally might have been as useful to me as the stones carried up long ago from the bed of the Jordan were to the Israelites who had passed over them dry-shod.'

William's life was now changed. Everything, from now on, was to become subservient to his mission to serve the God who had saved him.

The Nottingham Walk

This walk will take you on a journey from the house where William Booth was born on 10 April 1829 to various places connected with his early life, before he left for London in 1849. Please allow approximately two and a half hours for this walk.

We begin at the **William Booth Memorial Complex,** Nottingham Goodwill Centre, 14, Notintone Place, Sneinton, Nottingham, NG2 4QG. ☎ (0115) 950 3927. The Complex encompasses much of the Salvation Army work on the area, and includes the William Booth Birthplace Museum.

By car: Nottingham is 130 miles (210 km) from London. From Junction 24 (M1) Leave motorway (signposted Nottingham S) and at roundabout take 4th exit A453. **Ratcliffe-on-Soar Power Station** (on left) in 3.9 mi, at roundabout take 2nd exit. **(edge of) Clifton** in 1.1 mi branch left (signposted Grantham A52). **Junction with A52** at roundabout take 1st exit B680. In 0.3 mi at mini-roundabout

forward. **Junction with B680** at mini-roundabout forward (signposted West Bridgeford). **West Bridgeford** at traffic lights turn left A60 (signposted Nottingham). A60 **'Trent Bridge Inn'** at traffic lights turn right A6011 (signposted Grantham A 52). A6011 **(road to) Nottingham Forest Football Club (on left). Junction with Lady Bay Bridge** at traffic lights turn left. A6911 **Junction with Meadow Lane** turn right into Meadow Lane. At the end of Meadow Lane, turn left into Sneinton Hermitage, continuing into Manvers Street. On entering the one-way system bear right and turn right into Sneinton Road. The William Booth complex is approximately 0.5 mi on the left. There is a car park at the rear of the building.

By public transport: Bus—Routes 23, 23A and 24 from the City centre (King Street) stop near the William Booth Complex (alight at Windmill Street). Enquiries (Travelwise)

☎ 0845 6088 608. (Traveline) ☎ 0870 606 2 608 (0700 to 2100 hrs daily). By rail—Notintone Place is approximately 1 mile from Nottingham Railway Station. On leaving the station, walk down Station Road; turn left into London Road. At the roundabout take the last exit (right) into Poplar Street which becomes Evelyn Street. Turn left into Manvers Street and cross the road. Take first left into Newark Street and then the second left into Notintone Place. At the end of this road, at the junction with Sneinton Road is the William Booth Memorial Complex.

12 Notintone Place (viewing by appointment: ☎ 0115 950 3927)

This house, where William was born, contains the William Booth Birthplace Museum. Here is a mine of information on the life of William Booth, plus many interesting artifacts, not just on William, but on the history of The Salvation Army. (Viewing is by appointment)

On leaving the William Booth Complex cross Sneinton Road and turn left.

Left: Impressive, but now no longer in use as a place of worship, the former Albion Congregational Chapel opened in 1856 to seat 800

Facing page: Plaque outside Booth's birthplace

St Stephen's Church

William was baptized in this Church when he was two days old. Three churches have stood on

this site. The present building was erected when William was ten years old.

Walk back, downhill, along Sneinton Road. The imposing building on the left is the former Albion Chapel—opened in 1856. This Congregational chapel seated 800 people. It is no longer in use as a place of worship.

At the bottom of the hill, cross into Bath Street. Cut through the Sneinton Market on the left and cross Gedling Street into Brook Street (formerly Colwick Street). Turn left into Boston Street. On the corner is Sneinton House.

Sneinton House

This is a modern Salvation Army hostel for 220 men and provides a rehabilitation programme for alcoholics. It also acts as a bail hostel for men on remand from the courts.

Continue along Boston Street and turn right into Lower Parliament Street. Almost opposite is the site of the house in Kid Street.

The house in Kid Street

This is where William preached his first sermon. The house was situated on the site occupied by industrial premises next door to the Byron Works.

Turn back along Lower Parliament Street, crossing Boston Street and, at the traffic light, cross Lower Parliament Street into Hockley. Turn left into Belward Street. On the right, at the junction with Barker Gate, opposite the modern Nottingham Ice Centre, is a small clump of trees. This is the site of Frances Eames' Pawnbrokers.

Francis Eames' Pawnbrokers

William became an apprentice to Eames at the age of thirteen. The side door of the shop is in the Museum at 12 Notintone Place. It was here that William came to see the effects of poverty upon people. William worked here until his apprenticeship finished at the age of 19.

Return to Hockley and turn left into Goose Gate.

Goose Gate

After the death of William's father, Samuel, William's mother Mary Moss opened a small shop in Goosegate—selling lace and ribbons. Later on, his sisters Emma and Mary opened another shop at 5 Hockley.

Continue up the Goosegate and turn left into the short pedestrianized section of Stoney Street.

Stoney Street

Stopping at the corner and looking back across Stoney Street we can see Broad Street, where the Wesley Chapel stood. It was through Stoney Street that William used to bring the ragged youngsters from the 'Bottoms', one of the

poorest parts of Nottingham, to the Broad Street chapel.

Continue to the end of Stoney Street. On the right is The Parish Church of St Mary the Virgin.

The Parish Church of St Mary the Virgin

William's father, Samuel, married his first wife, Sarah Lockitt here, in 1797. The church building was in poor condition during William's childhood and was restored between 1843 and 1848.

Cut through the churchyard or (if the gates are shut) continue along the High Pavement (above).

At the main entrance to St Mary's turn right up the narrow St Mary's Gate. This takes us into the old Lace Market area of Nottingham. Turn left into Pilcher Gate. Opposite a

car park turn left into Halifax Place. On the right is Biddulph's Academy.

Biddulph's Academy

Now the Lace Market Theatre, this building was where William received much of his education. The Biddulph's were members of the Broad St Chapel. William left here at the age of thirteen to start work in Francis Eames' pawnbrokers shop.

Return to the end of Halifax Place and turn left into Pilcher Gate. At the end, turn right into Fletcher Gate. Turn right again into Carlton Street and take the second turning left into Broad Street, the site of The Wesley Chapel.

The Wesley Chapel

It was here that William was converted and from here started his early Christian work. Now the Broadway Cinema Complex, the building still retains the impressive pillars from the Wesley Chapel. Inside the foyer, on the left is a plaque commemorating William's conversion.

Continue down Broad Street. Turn left into Old Lenton Street and right into George Street. On the left is the office of Watson

Fothergill (Architect), an interesting old building that William would have been familiar with.

At the bottom of George Street at the junction with Lower Parliament Street is The Wesley Centre.

The Wesley Centre

This building contains a number of articles of interest taken from the Broad Street Chapel at its closure. The building now has a glass lean-to frontage which is used as a cafeteria.

Turn right into Lower Parliament Street. Cross at the traffic lights to 'The Palais' and continue down King Edward Street. At the bottom, on the right, is the imposing building of:

Memorial Halls

The William Booth Memorial Halls

This building was erected in 1915, and has a seating capacity of 750. It contains a portrait of William Booth, and has a tablet in the foyer celebrating his conversion.

Adjoining the premises is the Salvation Army Citadel.

Cross the road into Bath Street and St Mary's Rest Garden. Follow the main path, up the hill to:

Bendigo's Tomb

William Abednego Thompson was a reformed drunkard and prize-fighter, who after his conversion became an evangelist. This tomb reminds us of the transforming effect of the gospel that William Booth preached to the masses.

Continue through the double gates and turn

right along the path back to Bath Street. Turn left and continue to the bottom of the hill. At the traffic lights cross straight over into Sneinton Road. On the left, at the junction with West Walk is a small triangle of trees. On this site stood:

The Booth's third home

William lived here with his parents from 1835 to 1843, after they had returned from Bleasby.

Continue up Sneinton Road to the William Booth Memorial Complex.

Above: *The office of Watson Fothergill, a curious building in George Street that William would have known*

③ From pawnbroker to preacher

William Booth wasted no time in taking the gospel to the poor in Nottingham's busy streets. It was here that the pattern for his life's work was set. Occupied in the pawnbrokers for thirteen hours each working day, he devoted the rest of his waking time to evangelism. At the age of nineteen he set out for London and full-time Christian work

It was not long after his conversion that William displayed the qualities that would fit him for a life of Christian service. His new found zeal was sparked and kindled by his long-held boyhood friendship with Will Sansom, the son of a lace maker. The two young men had been close neighbours in early childhood. Brought up side by side in Notintone Place, the fortunes of their families had taken different directions. Whilst the Booths had spiralled down the social ladder into hardship, the Sansoms had continued to prosper. This, however, did not affect the deep friendship that continued to develop between them.

There is little doubt that at this time Will Sansom was the leader. He was a handsome, frail looking young man, already showing the signs of tuberculosis, a wasting disease that would shortly end his life. In contrast to his physical condition Will Sansom possessed a deep spiritual energy and zeal for the lost souls that surrounded them everywhere on the streets of Nottingham. After a long hard day's work in Eames' pawnbroker

Above: Kid Street, where Booth preached his first sermon in 1846

Facing page: The Thames looking towards the City

shop, William would join his friend in visiting the sick. Open-air meetings followed this and, after the singing of a hymn, people would be invited to a local cottage for an evangelistic service. At this time, they drew their inspiration from John Wesley. Later in life Booth recalled, 'To me there was one God, and John Wesley was his prophet'!

At one point, William became ill. As he slowly recovered his strength, a message from Will Sansom provided the medicine he needed. Sansom was starting a mission to the poor in the slums of Nottingham and he urged William to join him in the cause. He was soon on the road to recovery and joined his friend.

His first sermon

Shy and self-conscious, Booth was willing to work hard for the cause in any capacity, but was reluctant to take centre stage at any of the meetings. It was David Greenbury, a tall, bearded evangelist who had come to Nottingham from Yorkshire, who persuaded him that it was his duty to stand up and speak to the people about the state of their souls and to point them to Jesus Christ, the only one who was able to save them. William soon had his first opportunity to preach at a cottage in Kid Street—to a crowd that extended into the street.

By now William was feeling disillusioned with the Methodist Church to which he belonged. The gospel was being preached, and people were called forward during the services as a sign of their desire to become Christians, but William noticed that at all these services the poor were conspicuous by their absence. His

Left: The site of Kid Street today

Above: *The gardens, Wollaton Park, Nottingham*

family's ill fortune and his experiences in the pawnbrokers had given him an affinity with the poor and a desire for their salvation and welfare.

The sight of a woman beggar, who had become a familiar feature of the Goosegate landscape, and who daily had to endure the taunts and mockery of the local children, moved William and Will Sansom to action. They set about her rescue from this state of poverty and humiliation. With the help of friends they raised enough money to rent a little cabin as a permanent home, furnished it, and managed to make regular provision for her daily needs. William saw, even at this early age, that the gospel went hand in hand with a practical demonstration of Christ's compassion for sinners. When one of the early converts died, William organized what he described as the first Salvation Army funeral. He managed to persuade the chaplain of the Pump Street cemetery to allow him to take over at the graveside after the funeral rites had been performed. With the small group of mourners—most of them recent converts—supplemented by onlookers from surrounding cottages and streets, William led in the singing of hymns and prayers, exhorting them to turn to Christ.

A number of preachers made their mark on him during this period. One of them was Isaac Marsden, who regularly preached at the Broad Street Chapel, and who had been influential in William's conversion. It was Marsden who showed William the importance of simple parables in communicating the gospel to those with no education. Passing a

James Caughey

house one day, where the woman was hanging up her washing, Marsden cried out, 'I say, missus, if your heart is not washed cleaner than those clothes, you'll never get to heaven.'

An Irish American who came to preach at the Broad St Chapel in May 1846 also influenced William. James Caughey had been taking Britain by storm since his arrival in 1841. Later in 1846 he would visit Sunderland and Gateshead where remarkable scenes were recorded by local newspapers.

Caughey's visit to Nottingham had been preceded by three months of preparation. Encouraged by the reports of the evangelist's impact on other towns and cities, regular meetings were held to pray for blessing on his labours. As anticipation of his visit intensified, Caughey became a constant topic of conversation in the Methodist community. Expectation was high and, as far as William Booth was concerned, Caughey did not disappoint. Crowds attended the meetings and many responded to the evangelist's conversational style of preaching and his fervent appeals for decisions. Converts were received into the church and many long-standing members, stirred by Caughey's appeal for sanctification, re-dedicated their lives to Jesus Christ.

The effect upon William was electric. He was now convinced that results would inevitably follow if the right means of evangelism were employed. Recalling the events, he wrote, 'I

Left: Salvation Army Citadel, King Edward Street

Above: Statue of Robin Hood at Nottingham Castle. It was during the reign of Henry I (1100-35) that the earlier wooden castle was replaced by a stone one with high walls and towers

saw as clearly as if a revelation had been made to me from Heaven that success in spiritual work, as in natural operations, was to be accounted for, not on any abstract theory of Divine sovereignty, or favouritism, or accident, but on the employment of such methods as were dictated by common sense, the Holy Spirit, and the Word of God.'

From this account we can see the beginning of William's deeply held convictions on how the gospel should be presented. Influenced initially by Wesley's

Arminianism, and Charles Grandison Finney's *Lectures on Revival*, he was now committed to a form of evangelism shaped by the evangelist's adaptability in using methods and means that work. William had no doubts that it was the responsibility of the evangelist to capture the minds and hearts of his hearers. In doing so, all methods could be legitimately employed. For him, the key question was not, 'Are they biblical?' but, 'Are they effective?'

Early work

One of the most notable converts of this time was Besom Jack, a broom maker who lived locally. Although described as a 'humorous minded rascal', he was in reality a notorious drunk and wife-beater. Every penny earned from the selling of brooms went on alcohol. His lifestyle meant that the family was so poor that his wife was reduced to begging for tea-leaves from their neighbours. Besom Jack was transformed when he heard and responded to the message preached by William and his associates on the streets of Nottingham. He became an ardent follower of the street preachers, doing all in his power to bring their message to his former drinking companions. Converts like Besom Jack caused friction between William and the leaders of the Broad Street Wesleyan Chapel. Instead of encouraging him, they cautioned him that he was going too fast. Matters were brought to a head at a Sunday morning service.

The Bottoms was Nottingham's

Charles Grandison Finney (1792–1875)

Finney was born in Warren, Connecticut and raised in Oneida County, New York. He trained and practised as a lawyer in Adams, New York. He was converted in 1821, and gave up his law practice to become a preacher. In 1824 he was ordained into the Presbyterian ministry and conducted evangelistic missions throughout the Eastern United States. In 1832 he became pastor of Second Presbyterian Church, New York City, where he began his *Lectures on Revival*, which was published in 1835. In the same year he became Professor of Theology at Oberlin, Ohio, where he stayed for the rest of his life, serving as president from 1851–66.

Finney rejected the doctrines of George Whitefield and Jonathan Edwards, and his own contemporary, Asahel Nettleton, all of whom witnessed great revival in many places across America. They held that revivals were an extraordinary and sovereign work of God, awakening the church and profoundly affecting the surrounding community. While they preached the gospel to all men, they firmly believed that Christ had died for the elect; and that a person could only become a Christian through the regenerating work of the Holy Spirit. Finney regarded these as an obstacle to evangelism and, impatient with what he regarded as the lack of success amongst preachers of his generation, proposed 'new measures', emphasizing the ability and responsibility of man to yield to the truth of the gospel. He presented this truth in a direct, dramatic and personal manner, using simple language and illustrations. He taught that revival was a continuous movement that should be promoted and maintained by the obedient church. This, in effect, took the power to change men's hearts out of the hand of God and placed it firmly in the hand of man himself.

most notorious and poverty stricken district. William saw this as a challenge to him. Concerned that the poor did not have the opportunity to hear the gospel preached he decided to do something about it. The service was in full swing, the congregation was singing heartily as only the Methodists of their day could, and the minister, Rev. Samuel Dunn, was seated in his comfortable pulpit chair.

Suddenly, the main door of the Chapel opened and in marched a company of the most ragged of Nottingham's poor. Bringing up the rear and driving his reluctant company on, was the tall figure of the young William Booth. 'Wilful Will', as he was now dubbed, ushered his ragged army to the comfortable seats generally occupied by 'pew renters'. Some of the worshippers quickly moved to another part of the chapel to

Left: Stoney Street. It was through here that William brought the ragged youngsters from one of the poorest parts of Nottingham to the Broad Street Chapel

get away from the smell and the threat posed by fleas and lice. Others shuffled uncomfortably and continued to worship. As soon as the service was over, William was summoned to appear before Samuel Dunn and the Chapel leaders. He was left in no doubt as to where they stood on the matter. The poor were welcome in the Chapel, but they were to be brought in by another door, and were to sit behind a screen away from the more sensitive members of the congregation, on hard wooden pews that would not provide a safe haven for fleas.

William took the rebuke well but he realised that the Methodism that had captivated him when reading the life of his hero, John Wesley, had now changed; he still believed that it was the place where the gospel was being preached and where converts could be built up in their faith. It would not be too long, however, before he would find that he did not belong in any of the established churches.

Samuel Dunn was looking for a young man who would take over some of the responsibility for preaching in the village chapels that surrounded Nottingham and someone suggested William—he was duly summoned before the minister. When asked whether he felt that he would be able to preach, William informed the minister that he already did—on the streets of the city. 'By whose authority?' retorted Dunn. Again, the young man graciously accepted the elder's rebuke. This must have impressed Dunn, because it was not long before William was an accredited local preacher and happily found himself in remote villages each

Sunday preaching the gospel that he loved.

Throughout this time, he continued working in Francis Eames' pawnbrokers. He saw this as his main goal in life; confining his religious work to any spare time he might have. It was not long, however, before his religious beliefs brought him into conflict with Eames. Saturday was their busiest day. Although the shops were supposed to close at midnight, in reality, the work continued into the early hours of Sunday morning. William was not averse to hard work, but he objected to working on the Lord's Day. He approached Eames on the matter and told him that he was willing to work until midnight Saturday and would gladly resume at midnight on Sunday, but would not work on God's day. Eames told him that he would have to continue working until everyone else stopped. If he refused to do so, he would be dismissed. William was true to his word— and so was Eames. He was now out of work—though not for long. Within seven days he was back at his post because Eames had realized that here was his best worker and he could not afford to be without him. To William's surprise Eames even left him in charge of the business when he took his young bride to Paris for their honeymoon.

London calling

As his apprenticeship came to an end at the age of nineteen, William had to make a decision about his future. He was now once again unemployed. Samuel Dunn urged him to consider offering

Above: Kennington Common opposite the site of Filmer's Pawnbroker's shop

Left: *Mary Booth, William's mother. His move to London meant that she would be without her son's immediate support for the first time in over twenty years*

himself for the Methodist ministry. William did not feel that God was calling him to this, but had no idea what he should do with his life. Nothing seemed to be happening for him in Nottingham at this time, so he made the momentous decision to leave for London. For the first time in almost twenty years his mother would be without her son's immediate support. In London, William hoped to make his fortune and deliver his family from their struggle against poverty.

Obtaining work in London was not as easy as William had imagined. To his dismay he was forced into returning to the trade that he had grown to loathe in Nottingham. He became an assistant pawnbroker to William Filmer in Kennington, South London. Living on the premises, he described his condition as being that of a 'white slave'.

He began to attend Walworth Chapel—and it was not long before he was invited to preach regularly to what he considered to be 'a respectable but dull and lifeless congregation.' He also preached in various other parts of the city, often travelling as far as Greenwich, about eight miles from its centre. Not content with just preaching on Sundays, William took the message of salvation into the neighbouring streets. This was a different experience from his days in Nottingham where his friends supported him. These early days in London were the loneliest of William's life. The prospect of full-time Christian service was now embedded in his thoughts, although there seemed to be little opportunity for this within the confines of Wesleyan

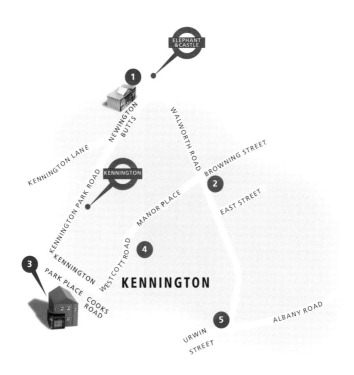

1 METROPOLITAN TABERNACLE
2 SITE OF EDWARD RABBIT'S HOUSE
3 SITE OF FILMER'S PAWNBROKERS
4 SURREY GARDENS

5 SITE OF WALWORTH CHAPEL
  (NOW CLUBLAND CHURCH)
6 SITE OF COOKE'S SEMINARY

Methodism. William was shortly to meet a man who would make his dream possible, and launch him into a sphere of Christian service that would have a world-wide impact.

Edward Harris Rabbits was a wealthy boot manufacturer who owned a chain of retail outlets. By 1851 he was reputed to be a millionaire! He was also an ardent supporter of the Reformers—a group within Methodism that sought to restore the movement to the ideals and practices of its founder, John Wesley. On a visit to Walworth Chapel, Rabbits heard William preach, and was moved by his earnestness and warmth, a quality that the Reformers felt had left Methodism with the coming of its social respectability. He invited the young preacher to dinner and it was not long before he began to speak to William about becoming a full-time preacher with the Reform movement: 'You must leave business, and wholly devote

Above: The Clubland church and centre, the site of the Walworth Chapel

yourself to preaching the gospel', Rabbits said. He asked William how much money he would need to do this. When William replied, 'Less than twelve shillings a week', the astute businessman retorted, 'Nonsense. You cannot do with less than twenty shillings a week.' William considered such matters to be merely academic until Rabbits broke the silence with: 'I will supply it for the first three months.' William's answer belied his enthusiasm: 'Very good', was all he said. He gave in his notice to the pawnbroker and began to plan for his day of freedom. The date fixed was Good Friday, 10 April 1852. It was William's twenty-third birthday.

Alongside these two things, there was something else that imprinted the day on his memory: 'On that day', he recalled, 'I fell over head and ears in love with the precious woman who afterwards became my wife.'

④ The love of his life

Good Friday 1852 was a momentous day for William Booth. It marked his entrance into full-time Christian service, and it was also the day on which he fell in love with Catherine—who later became the 'Mother' of The Salvation Army. Booth was sent to work in Spalding, Lincolnshire, and refined the methods of evangelism that he first began among the poor in Nottingham

Catherine Mumford was born in Ashbourne, Derby, on 17 January 1829, the only daughter of five children. Her father, a coach-builder, moved the family to Boston in Lincolnshire when she was five years old. From Boston they moved to Russell Street in what was then the leafy South London suburb of Brixton. Catherine was a serious child and deeply interested in spiritual matters. She is reputed to have read the Bible through eight times by the time she was twelve! Catherine was not a healthy child and never a healthy woman—although she bore seven children during her thirty-five year marriage to William. At the age of fourteen she developed curvature of the spine and incipient tuberculosis. Prolonged bouts of illness left her weak, but gave her time to read and think. She developed strong opinions on a number of issues including the use of alcohol, animal welfare, and women's rights.

Throughout her life Catherine was a strict teetotaller, and was prominent in the temperance movement. It is quite possible that

Above: Catherine Mumford pictured in her early twenties

Facing page: Picturesque Lincolnshire; William spent eighteen months in Spalding shortly after his engagement to Catherine

Left: The home of Edward Rabbits, where William Booth first met Catherine

Facing page: It was at a meeting of the Reformers in Cowper Street, just off the City Road, that William and Catherine met again. William offered to escort Catherine on the long carriage drive home to Brixton

these views stemmed from her relationship with her father, John Mumford who had been a local preacher and an activist in the temperance movement. He had, however, struggled with his faith and later it became sadly clear that he was drinking heavily. Catherine was deeply disturbed by this, and wrote, 'I sometimes get into an agony of feeling while praying for my dear father. O my Lord, answer prayer and bring him back to Thyself!' Catherine's prayer was heard, for in 1861 John Mumford showed signs of returning to the faith.

Even though she experienced intense religious convictions as a child, Catherine felt that she did not come into a living relationship with God until the age of sixteen, when she read the words of Charles Wesley's hymn: 'My God I am thine, what a comfort divine, What a blessing to know that my Jesus is mine!' It was then that she

felt assured of her salvation.

As a result of this experience, Catherine began to attend meetings of the Wesleyan Reformers in Brixton and it was not long before she was actively engaged in Sunday school work. It was here that Catherine first set eyes on William Booth. The Reformers held services at a hall in Binfield Road, Clapham and Catherine and her mother, Sarah, attended these services. One Sunday William came to preach and his text was chosen from the story of Jesus meeting the Samaritan woman at the well in Sychar. Catherine was impressed with the young preacher's earnestness and sincerity, and related this to Edward Rabbits, a long-time family friend. William does not record whether or not he noticed the pale skinned, dark haired, young lady in the congregation.

Love at first sight!

Two weeks later they met at a dinner party organised by Edward Rabbits. It was the very day that Rabbits confronted William with the call to full-time Christian service. A number of people were present and, to William's embarrassment, Rabbits urged him to recite the American poem, 'The Grog Seller's Dream.' It was not the most suitable poem for a dinner party in which wine would be served and controversy developed and conversations became heated. William was embarrassed, but he could not help noticing the young woman who seemed to revel in the anti-alcohol sentiments expressed in the poem! Catherine was not particularly attractive and her pale complexion was accentuated by the darkness of her hair, parted in the middle and bound together in buns. She had a small chin and a long nose. But it was the obvious depth of her faith, coupled with her forthright ability to express it, that impressed William.

They met again a few weeks later on Good Friday. It was William's twenty-third birthday and the day he was to launch himself into full-time Christian service. Both had attended a meeting of the Reformers in Cowper Street, just off the City Road. William offered to escort Catherine on the long carriage drive home to Brixton. During this journey they both realised that their feelings for each other had become more than simply admiration. They fell deeply in love and remained so throughout their marriage. Theirs was a true romance, but undergirding and directing their relationship was a heart-felt conviction that God had brought them together to fulfil his purpose for their lives and advance the cause of his kingdom. This is evident from their prolific letter-writing during their courtship and engagement. Catherine's letters eloquently portrayed their relationship. Typically, William's replies are more to the point, but it is clear that the bond between them was already strong. She was able to combine the role of star-struck lover and wise spiritual counsellor. On Saturday 15 May 1852 William and Catherine were engaged.

During the first few months of their engagement, from May through to October, they were uncertain about the direction in which their future work together would take. William was frustrated with his role among the

Reformers. He was successful in what he was doing, but felt that the Reform ministers were not adequately dealing with the converts that were produced by his ministry. He also felt that he was not given enough opportunities to preach. There seemed to him to be too much infighting within the denomination. Catherine suggested that they join with the Congregationalists and that William should apply to become a Congregational minister.

The Congregationalists were from a different rootstock to the Methodists. Their history was one of independence from the Established Church, with each congregation having the right to make its own decisions. The churches were loosely joined together in a union. This appealed to William and it was not long

before his application for the Congregational ministry was being considered. He was counselled to study and prepare himself for entry into the Cotton End Seminary, and was instructed to read two books that would help him understand the main thrust of the Congregational doctrines. These books, Payne's, *Divine Sovereignty* and *Reign of Grace* proved to be a stumbling block. William, who was never a theologian, could not understand how a man could hold to the doctrines of Calvinism and, at the same time, preach a gospel that invited *all* men to come to Christ. He struggled with this and soon found that he could not continue with his application. William read Payne and threw the book against the wall in disgust. He could not see that Calvinism, far from

ROBERT DALE

Above: Spalding, Lincolnshire

Above: Booth began a fruitful ministry in Spalding with his labours taking him to many villages. In his twenty-seven mile wide parish in the Methodist circuit he often preached in chapels like this

preventing whole hearted evangelism, actually spurred many men to preach to the masses. Significantly, two of England's greatest evangelists, George Whitefield—a contemporary of John Wesley, and Charles Haddon Spurgeon, one of Booth's own contemporaries, had little difficulty reconciling themselves to this doctrine.

Spalding

The Wesleyan Reformers solved Williams's dilemma. A Methodist circuit in Spalding, Lincolnshire, was looking for a minister and William, with Catherine's blessing, took up the challenge. He was to remain there for eighteen months, and despite being apart from his fiancée, he described this as being the happiest period of his ministry.

On arriving in Spalding, William threw himself wholeheartedly into the work. His labours took him to many villages in his twenty-seven mile wide parish. On the first Sunday fourteen people came forward to the communion rail in response to his appeal for converts. Such scenes followed almost every meeting he conducted while he was at the Spalding Circuit.

It was here that William began to refine the methods of evangelism that he had begun in the streets and cottages of Nottingham and during his time with the Reformers in London. Inspired by Finney, and urged on by Catherine's letters, he introduced the penitent form into his meetings. This was simply a bench, or a row of seats, placed in front of the preacher, where those

Calvinism

The term 'Calvinism' is used by various groups to identify their beliefs with one of the leaders of the reformation, John Calvin (1509–1564). Calvin believed that the doctrine and practice of the church should be founded solely on what the Bible teaches. Calvinism, sometimes called 'The Reformed Faith' or 'The Doctrines of Grace', principally addresses five particular points involving man's salvation. The five points are:

'Total depravity.' Every part of man's being is corrupted and enslaved by sin. It is the common grace of God that restrains him from exercising his full evil nature and enables him to do good. This includes the free will that he was given before the fall, thus rendering him incapable of saving himself.

'Unconditional election.' Before the foundation of the world, God chose to save undeserving sinners for salvation, not through any merit of their own, or because he foresaw their faith, but simply through his own electing grace.

'Limited Atonement.' The atonement is limited only in the sense that Christ's sacrifice for sin is effective for the elect alone. The atonement is complete and the debt for sin has been paid for all whom God has chosen to eternal life.

'Irresistible grace.' Although the elect may, for a time, resist God's saving grace, in the end their hostility and opposition will be removed, making them willing to embrace Christ. This is just as much a divine work as creation, whereby a man is born again by the Spirit of God.

'Perseverance of the saints.' The elect are eternally secure in Christ. Because salvation is God's work alone, he will keep his elect from falling away and ensure that they will persevere in this life until they are presented before the presence of his glory.

seeking salvation were invited to kneel and publicly demonstrate their desire to abandon their sinful lives and make their commitment to Jesus Christ. He would pray with each penitent, names and addresses would be taken, and they would be visited during the coming week so that enquiries could be made as to the state of their spiritual health. William was earnest in his desire to use all means for the conversion and sanctification of those to whom God had entrusted him with their spiritual welfare. Many who disagreed with his theology and methods could not but admire the young evangelist's earnestness and hard work in pastoral care.

At Swineshead Bridge, a small town in the Spalding district, William conducted a weeklong mission where he records that people wept bitterly and sought God's mercy. It was here that he felt that he had discovered the right approach to evangelism. He

Above: In 1939, over 100,000 acres of field around Spalding were given over to tulip cultivations compared to just 200 acres today. Much of the tulip growing in Lincolnshire goes on out of sight of the motorist

described it as the 'week which most effectually settled my conviction for ever that it was God's purpose by my using the simplest means to bring souls into liberty, and to break into the cold formal state of things to which His people are only too ready to settle down.'

Numerous letters passed between William and Catherine during this time. They spoke, not just of their great affection for each other, but were also full of their mutual desire to become a united means through which God could change people's lives.

There was one note of disagreement, however, that in many relationships could have led to a division. It was the matter of the role of women in the church. This was brought about by a sermon preached by the Reverend David Thomas, the minister of the Stockwell Congregational Church, which Catherine attended. In her opinion Thomas: 'appeared to imply the doctrine of women's intellectual or even moral inferiority to man.' Catherine was furious and in a long, unsigned letter made the minister aware of her views. This would be the first of many letters and pamphlets that would flow from her pen on this subject concerning the equality of women, not just in the home but also in the pulpit! On reading of this, William was somewhat taken aback, but in a conciliatory reply, he wrote, 'I would not encourage a woman to begin preaching', but then added, 'although I would not stop her on any account... I would not stop you if I had power to do so, although I should not like it.'

Later, in Gateshead, William would be faced with the practical reality of his reply!

A new direction

Towards the end of his ministry in Spalding, William and Catherine had become disillusioned with the Reformers. The movement was dogged by disputes and arguments and, with no central government, was unable to exercise the true Methodist discipline that William thought essential to its well being. As a result of this, he felt that his own ministry was going nowhere. Catherine shared his concerns and they both turned their attention towards another branch of Methodism—the New Connexion—which sought a more radical form of church government, introducing lay people into the decision making process. This appealed to both William and Catherine. William tried to persuade the leaders of the Spalding Circuit to join this emerging branch of Methodism, but in spite of their deep admiration and respect for him and the fear that they would lose this dynamic young preacher, they were cautious and would not come to a hasty decision. William saw no alternative but to leave Spalding and apply for entrance into the New Connexional ministry. He did so, was accepted for training, and returned to London on 14 February 1854. The next day he started at Dr William Cooke's seminary in Albany Road, Camberwell, not far from where he had previously lived in the Walworth Road.

Funded by Edward Rabbits, who had followed him into the New Connexion, William commenced his studies. Meanwhile, less than two miles away, in New Park Street, Southwark, another young man

Above: Burgess Park now occupies the site of the former Seminary where William Booth began training for the Methodist New Connexion ministry

Left: CH Spurgeon, a contemporary of Booth, aged 30 in 1864
Right: William Booth aged 30 in 1859

was beginning a ministry in London that would have world-wide repercussions. Charles Haddon Spurgeon had arrived in London from the fenlands of East Anglia. Booth and Spurgeon were different in temperament, theology and practice, but both made a notable impact for Christ on Victorian society—and both have left a lasting legacy. Further information on Spurgeon can be found in *Travel with Spurgeon*, in this series.

Dr Cooke, the college principal, was a celebrated scholar, and probably the most influential figure in the history of the New Connexion movement. Catherine was delighted that William had become a student and urged him on in his studies. William however, soon had reservations. He could not see how grappling with Latin and Greek, logic and rhetoric, would have any purpose in the work to

which God had called him. William Booth was primarily a man of action rather than a thinker. It was this drive and determination that God used in the founding of a great Christian movement.

One incident was instrumental in hastening William's entrance into the New Connexional ministry. At some point in a student's training, the college principal would attend a service where the student was preaching and the next day give a critique of the sermon. Dr Cooke went to hear William preach. William was on the horns of a dilemma as he spotted the principal and his family in the congregation. Desperately wanting to make a good impression, he was also aware that his commission from God was to preach the gospel to the lost. Describing the scene later, he wrote, 'I am not ashamed to say that I wanted to stand well with

Left: The statue of the father of Methodism, John Wesley gazes across from Wesley's Chapel, City Road, London

him. I knew also that my simple, practical style was altogether different from his own, and from the overwhelming majority of the preachers he was accustomed to approve… *but* I saw dying souls before me, the gates of Heaven wide open on the one hand, and the gates of Hell open on the other, while I saw Jesus Christ with His arms open between the two, crying out to all to come and be saved. My whole soul was in favour of doing what it could to second the invitation of my Lord, and doing it that very night.' Forsaking homiletic principles, William preached in his usual simple, but somewhat eccentric style. At one point he jumped onto the pulpit seat and waved his handkerchief round and round in a dramatic gesture. At the close of the sermon he gave an appeal. One of those who came forward was Cooke's daughter. Dr Cooke was a grateful man and he was also a wise man. The next day William went to his study for the critique of the sermon. 'My dear sir', said Dr Cooke, 'I have only one thing to say to you, and that is, go on in the way you have begun, and God will bless you.'

Within a year, William was accepted as a probationary minister and appointed Deputy Superintendent of the London Circuit. This released him to do the work to which he firmly believed that he had been called. During this time he preached as far afield as Guernsey, Bristol, Newcastle and Manchester. In June of that year, William and Catherine embarked upon the next stage of their life and ministry together.

Above: Binfield Road, Stockwell

TRAVEL INFORMATION

The Congestion Charge and difficulty with parking make it advisable to use public transport when travelling in Central London.

Stockwell New Chapel SW9

Situated in Stockwell Green, just off Stockwell Road. The chapel where William and Catherine Booth were married still stands. It is now a mosque and Khatme Natuwwat Islamic centre.
By car: parking in side streets (very limited)
By public transport: Underground: Stockwell or Brixton (Victoria Line). Bus service: 2; 88; 322; 345.

Binfield Road SW4

Binfield House, a Reformers Hall in Binfield Road, is where Catherine Mumford first heard William Booth preach. He spoke from John 4:42 'This is indeed the Christ, the Saviour of the world.' The hall has long been demolished.

Russell Street (now Hillyard Street) SW9

Catherine Mumford lived here when she first met William Booth. It was to this street that they returned on the carriage ride from Cowper Street, EC2, when they realised their love for each other. The original buildings have been demolished and newer houses stand in their place. Not far away is St Anne's Terrace (now Southey Road) where Susannah Thompson (later to become Mrs CH Spurgeon) lived. See *Travel with Spurgeon*, published by Day One.
By public transport: Underground—Victoria Line to Brixton. Bus service—3 from Oxford Circus; 59 from Euston; 133 from Liverpool Street; 159 from Marble Arch.

Albany Road SE5

At 3, The Crescent was William Cooke's Seminary where William Booth began training for the Methodist New Connexion ministry. The whole site is now taken up by Burgess Park.

HILLYARD ST

SOUTH LAMBETH ROAD

A3 CLAPHAM ROAD

BINFIELD ROAD

STOCKWELL

STOCKWELL

A3 CLAPHAM ROAD

STOCKWELL GARDENS

STOCKWELL ROAD

SIDNEY ROAD

A 23 BRIXTON ROAD

STOCKWELL NEW CHAPEL

STOCKWELL PK WLK

A 23 BRIXTON ROAD

BRIXTON

1 HILLYARD STREET (FORMERLY RUSSELL ST) WHERE CATHERINE MUMFORD LIVED WHEN SHE FIRST MET WILLIAM BOOTH
2 BINFIELD ROAD WHERE CATHERINE FIRST HEARD WILLIAM PREACH IN THE HALL USED BY THE WESLEYAN REFORMERS
3 STOCKWELL NEW CHAPEL (NOW A MOSQUE) WHERE WILLIAM AND CATHERINE MARRIED

Left: The site of Filmer's Pawnshop Kennington Park Road

Below: Spalding, where William preached for eighteen months. Modern Spalding now has busy markets, and a traditional shopping centre

Walworth Chapel SE5

This site on the corner of Camberwell Road and Grosvenor Terrace (almost opposite Albany Road) is now occupied by the Clubland Methodist Church and Centre. William Booth preached at the Walworth Chapel, and it was here that he met Edward Rabbits.

Rabbits' House SE17

199 Walworth Road (formerly Crosby Road). The house stands on the corner of Browning Street. It was here that William Booth and Catherine Mumford met at a dinner party and where William recited the poem, 'The Grog Seller's Dream'.

Filmer's Pawnshop SE11

176, Kennington Park Road (formerly 1, Kennington Row). This is where William Booth was first employed when he came to London in 1849. Opposite is Kennington Park (formerly Kennington Common) where George Whitefield preached.

Spalding

The home to William and Catherine Booth for eighteen months, Spalding, Lincolnshire is a small market town of about 20,000 residents and stands midway between Boston and Peterborough. Spalding is an important agricultural town and the centre of the

flower industry—more daffodils are grown there than any other part of Britain.

Modern Spalding now has busy markets, a traditional shopping centre and the new Holland Markets retail area.

For travel information about places to visit, events, attractions, festivals, local accommodation, transport, walks and cycle routes, call 01775 725 468 Website: www.sholland.gov.uk

⑤ A remarkable marriage

William and Catherine Booth began their married life working in the north of England. In Gateshead, crowds flocked to hear William preach, and controversy broke out when Catherine, by now a mother, announced her own call to be a preacher. Leaving the confines of denominational life, they travelled to Cornwall and saw many lives changed through their ministry

William and Catherine were married on 17 June 1855 at Stockwell New Chapel in South London. After a week's honeymoon on the Isle of Wight, just off the coast of southern England, they travelled to Guernsey in the Channel Islands, for a series of mission meetings. Catherine was delighted that she was now able to join William in his campaigns. She was not a good sailor, however, and was frequently sick. On their return to London Catherine was too ill to journey north with her husband—but was soon able to join him towards the end of his campaign in Hull, a busy seaport on the North East coast. Unfortunately she was ill again, and stayed with some friends in Caistor, where she gathered enough strength to join him again as he travelled to Sheffield. The short stay in the 'steel city' was a happy time for them both. William preached to packed chapels and there were many converts.

By October 1855, only four months after their wedding,

Above: The former Stockwell New Chapel where William and Catherine were married in 1855— now a Mosque

Facing page: William and Catherine, Penzance 1862

William's methods of evangelism were beginning to cause ripples of discontent among the New Connexionalists. Some of the ministers thought that William's emotionally charged sermons and appeals for conversions were producing shallow results. Undaunted by criticism, the Booths continued their tour of the northern towns and cities with great success. At the last meeting of a month's campaign in Dewsbury, Yorkshire, over two thousand people packed into the local chapel to hear William preach.

Catherine was unwell again and she was also expecting their first child. At the end of the year they made the short journey to Leeds where, in two months, over eight hundred conversions were recorded. This was followed by another month's campaign in Halifax. It was here, on 8 March 1856 that William Bramwell was born.

Campaigns in Sheffield, Chester, Truro, and a short tour of the Midlands, including William's home city of Nottingham, brought William to prominence within the New Connexion. Many were extolling his virtues as an eccentric but effective evangelist, while others were becoming increasingly disturbed by his methods. At the New Connexion conference in June 1857, it was agreed to appoint William as the circuit superintendent at Brighouse in Yorkshire. Unhappy at a decision that would, in effect, clip his wings, William saw no alternative other than to obey. The Booths travelled to the town to settle in their first permanent home since their marriage. By now, Catherine was expecting their second child.

Above: Brighouse was a textile town that grew along the canal, which ran through the town. The town played an important part in shaping the Booths' future work with the poor

William Bramwell Booth (1856–1929)

Although different in character from his father, Bramwell Booth worked faithfully alongside him in the work of The Salvation Army. His organizational skills were essential to the growth of the Army during his father's lifetime. In 1882 he married Florence Soper, a fellow Salvation Army officer who had worked with his sister Kate in Paris. Florence was the organiser of the Women's Social Work. Their seven children all followed their parents into the work. Their daughter Catherine became one of the Army's most influential and popular Commissioners.

From 1880 to 1912 Bramwell was the Army's Chief of Staff, and succeeded his father as General from 1912 to 1929. Under his leadership the Army emphasized the doctrine of holiness and expanded its world wide mission. Bramwell Booth was honoured by the nation—being made a Companion of Honour shortly before his death in 1929. He was buried in Abney Park cemetery—his coffin bearing the Companion of Honour motto, 'in action faithful, in honour clear'

Brighouse

Brighouse was a town that grew out of textile production. Traffic on the canal, which ran through the town, made its way across the Pennines from Liverpool in the west to Hull in the east. The Booths felt that the town was unattractive and they considered the potential for William's ministry to be even less so. He was, by now, used to success. Everywhere he went there were enthusiastic crowds and many conversions. Brighouse was another matter!

On 28 July 1857 their second son, Ballington was born. Unlike Bramwell he was of a fiery nature; but like Bramwell he too would become an integral part of the Salvation Army's work. In 1881 he was put in charge of the Army's first training home and he was later sent to the United States to oversee the Army's work. In 1896, after a disagreement with his father, he and his wife, Maud, resigned and established their own movement. Ballington died in 1940 at the age of eighty-three. The time spent in Brighouse did, however, play an important part in shaping the Booths' future work. Catherine was brought face to face with the problems experienced by the poor. This prompted a life-long campaign for better working conditions for young women. She also began a more public ministry of her own, setting up Bible classes for women and children.

For both William and Catherine, there was one ray of light in the darkness they felt had descended upon them at

Brighouse. James Caughey had returned to England, and in February they travelled to Sheffield to hear him preach and, hopefully, to meet him. They were not disappointed. Caughey greeted them warmly and William was able to seek the counsel of one of his heroes. Surprisingly, Caughey, who was as independently minded and headstrong as William, urged them to be patient. William's probationary period would soon be over, and as a fully ordained minister he would be better equipped and able to pursue any avenue in which his future work would take. The Booths accepted the evangelist's advice and, before returning to Brighouse, Caughey baptized Ballington.

Gateshead

At the New Connexion spring conference William was ordained, and the couple were sent to Gateshead, a town situated on the north-east Coast of England, across the river Tyne from Newcastle. In Tyneside, both William and Catherine's future work would emerge from the chrysalis, and the wings that would carry it to the furthermost parts of the earth would unfold. John Wesley had frequently visited the area, establishing and nurturing Methodist societies. In 1836, the New Connexion had built Bethesda Chapel in Melbourne Street, in the Barns Close area of the town. Built to hold twelve hundred worshippers, the church had never really fulfilled its potential, and when

Below: Bethesda Chapel nicknamed, 'The Converting Shop'

Right: Created by sculptor Antony Gormley, The Angel of the North rises 65 feet (20 metres) over the hilltop landscape. It marks the southern entry to Tyneside and is on the edge of the Great North Forest

William took up his post, there were only ninety members—and at least half of these were just nominal.

Catherine felt instinctively that Gateshead was going to be a good place to live and work. She was also expecting their third child—a daughter—who was born three months after their arrival. Catherine ('Katie'), named after her mother, followed her brothers into almost legendary status in The Salvation Army. She was given the formidable task of taking the Army's work to Paris, where she received the name 'La Marechale'—the Field Marshal. Their second daughter, Emma Moss Booth, was born on 8 January 1860. In 1903, having been sent to the United States to replace her brother Ballington as the leader of the American work, she was tragically killed in a train crash.

The Booths threw themselves enthusiastically into their work. It was not long before William was conducting open-air meetings in the streets or in the nearby Windmill Hills where they lived. Catherine, appalled by the poverty and drunkenness of so many of Gateshead's population, began to visit the cramped back-to-back houses that were a feature of the town. William was now in his element. Crowds were flocking to hear him preach, many conversions were recorded, and the membership of Bethesda Chapel was rapidly growing. Such was his impact on the town that

Above: Catherine Booth preaching at the City Temple, London. She preached her last sermon here in 1888

the Chapel was given the nickname, 'The Converting Shop'!

It was in Gateshead that Catherine became a preacher. At Pentecost in 1860 as William was closing the morning service at Bethesda, he looked up and saw Catherine walking towards him: 'I want to say a word', she said to her astonished husband. William did not try to prevent her and turning to the congregation who were by now perplexed by what was happening, he said, 'My dear wife wishes to speak.' Catherine slowly mounted the pulpit steps and William nervously sat down. Addressing the congregation, she told them of how she had felt a call to preach, but for fear of being considered a fool had persistently resisted it: 'I have not yet been willing to be a fool for Christ. Now I will be one.' The congregation was stunned. Some were undoubtedly angry that a woman was standing in their pulpit, let alone announcing her

call to preach! Others wept, obviously moved by Catherine's bravery and honesty. William seized the moment and leaping to his feet he announced in a strong tone: 'Tonight, my wife will be the preacher!' For the rest of their lives, neither Catherine nor William doubted that this was God's call to the Christian ministry, not just for Catherine, but for many women who would follow in her footsteps.

It was also in Gateshead that Catherine claimed to be 'sanctified'. John Wesley had taught the doctrine of Christian perfection. Finney had written about it, James Caughey had preached it, and it had been an integral part of the teaching of the Methodism into which William had been converted and in which he served.

There is no doubt that in the matter of women preaching and the doctrine of Christian perfection, Catherine and William were influenced by the visit to Tyneside in 1859 of the American evangelist Phoebe Palmer who had caused a stir among the more conservative Christians in the area. It also brought intense opposition from local ministers. One wrote a scathing attack upon the evangelist, causing Catherine to publish a pamphlet defending this kindred spirit. William's wholehearted support for his wife in this matter brought opposition to the Booths within the New Connexion. Coupled with this was their deep concern for the poor, whom they felt were still being neglected by the church at large and by their own denomination in particular.

Independence beckons

Matters came to a head at the May 1861 conference in Liverpool when many within the denomination felt that the Booths were doing a great work in Gateshead, but other— more influential—figures differed. During the period leading up to the conference William had been ill, and Catherine had taken charge of his duties. She was, in the eyes of many, acting as an ordained New Connexion minister. The cause of controversy that eventually led to the Booths' resignation, was a letter from William requesting a change of status and duties within his denomination. He was convinced that God wanted him to be an evangelist but the denomination had no such office, and they had no intention of creating it just for him! Such was the Booths' status that a large proportion of conference time was given over to debating the issue. A compromise was offered. William could be appointed superintendent of the Newcastle Circuit, with permission to conduct periodic evangelistic campaigns in other parts of the country.

The Booths were now facing a dilemma. They were people of high principle; but they were also the parents of four children.

Christian perfection

Sanctification is a theological term sometimes used in conjunction with 'Christian perfection' and 'holiness.' Biblically, it has two main meanings. First, it refers to the righteousness of Jesus Christ reckoned (credited) to the life of the believer, and secondly it refers to the Christian's growth into Christ's likeness. John Wesley, however, held the view that moral or religious perfection is not just the ideal to which the Christian must strive, but that it was an attainable goal in this life. He also taught that it could be instantaneously received by faith and confirmed by the witness of the Holy Spirit. For Wesley, Christian perfection or 'holiness' was an experience that set the Christian free from sins that were 'voluntary transgressions of a known law.' This does not mean that the 'sanctified' can be perfect in knowledge or understanding, as God is perfect; neither does it mean that, in this life, he or she can be made absolutely perfect.

Apart from the New Connexion they had no home and no income. To truly obey God, they must honour his call, but also they must honour their parental responsibilities. They did not act hastily or foolishly. William obediently took up the work in Newcastle, knowing, however, that this was the beginning of the end. Many doors within the New Connexion were closing to him. Both William and Catherine saw this as a time to seek God's will. In July, William received a reprimand claiming that he had failed to take up his proper pastoral work in Newcastle. William felt he had no choice but to resign.

The Booth family was shortly to be homeless and penniless in Victorian Britain—the Welfare State was almost a hundred years away. However, any feelings of apprehension were swamped by a deep sense of liberation. The shackles were now loose.

Cornwall

In July 1861 the Booths moved to London to stay with Catherine's parents and await God's next move. The call was not long in coming. William and Catherine were invited to preach over a seven-week period in Hayle, Cornwall. Leaving their children with the Mumfords, the couple set out on the long journey from London, and on 11 August began a work that would last for eighteen months.

Cornwall had witnessed revival in the past. John Wesley had been a frequent visitor to the county and so, once again William was following in his hero's footsteps. In Hayle, the Booth's witnessed some amazing scenes. The town and its surrounding area seemed to be enveloped by a sense of

Above: St. Ives. When the Booths started ministering in Cornwall, converts openly displayed their joy to passers by

Left: Wherever the Booths went, ordinary people were open to the message, but established churches invariably found fault.
Pictured: William and Catherine in 1860

God's presence. Fishermen rowed across choppy seas and villagers walked miles to hear the gospel preached. On the streets, converts openly displayed their joy to passers by. Many other Cornish towns and villages experienced the same phenomena wherever the Booths ministered. In St Ives, two local dignitaries and twenty-eight fishermen were converted. In St Just, the local police inspector reported a dramatic drop in crime, and publicans reported a large fall in trade. In the midst of the campaign both William and Catherine were unwell. At one point William suggested to Catherine that he should return to London and seek some kind of commercial work.

William's methods were also a matter of concern to some local Methodist ministers. The introduction of the 'penitent form' and the unbridled enthusiasm of the meetings were considered to be, if not irreverent, at least inappropriate. Doors began to close. It seemed that the same old pattern was developing. Wherever the Booths went, the common people accepted them with open arms, but it was never long before the established churches found fault and tried to curb their activities.

The campaign continued until August 1862. Both William and Catherine missed their children, whom they had left in London, anticipating only a seven-week parting. Before they were reunited there was another addition to the family. Catherine gave birth to Herbert on 26

Above: In Hayle, fishermen rowed across choppy seas and villagers walked miles to hear the gospel preached

August. Herbert became a talented musician, writing a number of the Salvationists' songs. He was later made principal of the Army's men's training home, and worked in Canada and Australia.

By now the New Connexion had officially accepted William's resignation. In January 1863, campaigns were held in Cardiff, the capital city of Wales. Many of the churches were now closed to them, forcing them to hold meetings in hired halls and even a disused circus tent! On leaving Cardiff the Booths campaigned in the West Midlands. In Walsall,

Above: *Lands End. Cornwall had witnessed revival in the past. The Booths spearheaded a ministry which had a huge impact across a wide area*

William learned to use sensational publicity and the personal testimony of 'notorious' converts in attracting people to his meetings. Those who would not come to hear an ordained preacher sat enthralled as a converted prize fighter or ex-poacher spoke of their conversion to Christ.

Needing to find a settled home for their five children, they moved to Leeds, in West Yorkshire, where both William and Catherine were able to preach. On 4 May 1864, their sixth child was born. Marian Billups Booth, named after a friend from their Cardiff days,

was a life-long invalid, who rarely left the Booth household. Her last public appearance was at William's funeral in 1912.

By now, it would be true to say that Catherine was a more popular preacher than William. She was increasingly receiving invitations to preach in London. A Londoner by nature, she wrote to her mother: 'I should like to live in London, better than any place I was ever in.' By early 1865, Catherine's wish and God's will had coincided when she was invited to take a mission in Rotherhithe, in the south east part of the city.

⑥ 'I have found my destiny!'

On an East London street, William Booth discovered the work that was to consume the rest of his life. As founder and head of the Christian Mission—later to become the Salvation Army—he reached out to the destitute and desperate in one of the poorest areas of the capital. The Mission rapidly expanded as others joined him

In February 1865 the Booths moved to London. They were by now in their mid-thirties with six children. With William's support, Catherine accepted an invitation to preach at a mission in Rotherhithe, in London's docklands on the south bank of the Thames. Her reputation had also reached the more affluent chapels in the West End of the capital. William was conducting a campaign in Lincolnshire and although he did not feel a deep sense of call to the capital, he agreed that it would be best for the whole family to move down from Leeds and make their base in London. They rented 31 Shaftesbury Road, a large family house in Hammersmith, West London. William headed back to Yorkshire to take a short mission in the cathedral city of Ripon. Every day, until the late spring, Catherine would make the long, exhausting, journey across the River Thames, to the rough and dangerous dockland areas, often returning home well after midnight.

Meanwhile, William had returned to London with the idea

Above: The Blind Beggar in Whitechapel. It was near this building William Booth stopped on a July evening, and preached the gospel

Facing page: The City of London. During 1865, Catherine Booth preached at a mission at Rotherhithe in the docklands

Above: Piccadilly, in the West End of London. Catherine preached in the affluent chapels around this area

Facing page: The bust of William Booth at Whitechapel

Above: Catherine Booth in her 30s

that this would be his base for further missions throughout the country. It was not long, however, before he too was brought face to face with the poverty and vice that infected the millions who thronged the narrow streets, and lived in the hovels that were packed tightly together in poorer parts of the city.

The mission begins

The Blind Beggar public house stands on the corner of Whitechapel Road and Cambridge Heath Road. Running east is Mile End Road, a busy route in and out of the City of London. Somewhere near this building, on what was then the Mile End Waste, William Booth stopped on a July evening, and preached the gospel. He had been invited to take part in a tent mission on the nearby disused Quaker burial ground in Baker's Row. Looking at the mass of poor, often derisive, people he said, 'There is a Heaven in East London for everyone—for everyone who will stop and think and look to Christ as a personal Saviour.' William later recorded: 'When I saw those masses of poor people, so many of them evidently without God or hope in the world, and found that they so readily and eagerly listened to me… I walked back to our West-End home and said to my wife, "O Kate, I have found my destiny!"'

William threw himself wholeheartedly into the work. Almost every day, he would walk eight miles from Hammersmith to preach in the open air on the Mile End Waste. He would frequently preach outside the Vine Tavern and invite interested hearers to the tent mission. There were many converts, and as the Mission grew, so did the opposition. This often resulted in violent action, and William would make his way back to Shaftesbury Road bruised and bloodied.

One of those early converts was Peter Monk, a prize-fighter. One evening, this tough Irishman had been on his way to a match on a small plot of land behind the Blind Beggar. On the street outside he met William Booth who told him about the work he was doing, that he was preaching nearby, and invited him to attend. Later as an old man, the Irishman used to recall that there was something about that

conversation with William that compelled him to give up his old life and follow Jesus Christ. The following evening, he was due to fight another Irishman, by the name of FitzGerald and Monk feared that his opponent would not only beat him, but also inflict heavy injuries upon him. Monk's heart was not in the fight, but he chose to go ahead. To his amazement he won easily. After the fight he lost no time in making his way to the tent where William was preaching—surrounded by what Monk described as, 'the greatest vagabonds you could meet anywhere on God's earth.' William's words were being greeted with ribald laughter, and it was almost impossible for him to be heard above the din. Monk threw off his coat, rolled up his sleeves and paraded up and down the aisles. Within two minutes the congregation was 'as quiet as lambs'. Peter Monk too, had found his destiny on the Mile End Waste, and God had now provided William with a bodyguard!

Everything seemed to be moving at a whirlwind pace. The tent meetings were packed and every night people from all kinds of backgrounds were seeking salvation. The Booths were now in need of money; not just for themselves, but also to continue and expand their work. Their weekly income was just three pounds and they were barely able to provide for themselves and their six children, let alone help the thousands of poor and destitute that surrounded them in London's East End. William was becoming exhausted by his long journey across the city.

While William confined his efforts to the East End of London, Catherine's reputation grew in the wealthier chapels in the West End and it was the income from her ministry that supported the family. William also made contact with Samuel Morley, a wealthy textile manufacturer, who was the Liberal Member of Parliament for Nottingham. As the work grew, many other wealthy businessmen joined the Booths in their crusade against poverty and vice.

Family life

In November 1865 the family moved to 1 Cambridge Villas, Hackney, about a mile north of Whitechapel. On Christmas Day, Catherine gave birth to their seventh and last child, Eveline Cory. A fiery redhead, she was always known as Eva and, on becoming Commander of the Salvation Army in the United States, she was persuaded to take the name Evangeline. Eva spent most of her working life in America, eventually taking citizenship there. In 1934 she became the first woman General of The Salvation Army. She died in New York in 1950.

William was now able to spend more time at home with his family. He would take part in, and often instigate games of 'Fox and Geese' and other boisterous childhood favourites. When they had exhausted themselves, they would sit down and play the popular card game, 'Snap'. The Booth household was orderly and the children were strictly and lovingly disciplined. Prayer was a natural part of the daily routine. Apart from family devotions, William and Catherine prayed with their children whenever there was cause

Above: Sundial erected on the site of the tent in the Quaker burial ground

Above: Salvation Army, Cambridge Heath Citadel, near the site of Cambridge Villas, Hackney

to punish them, or whenever there was need to encourage or comfort them. Although they lived above the poverty line, the Booths had little money. The children were sent to school with patches on their clothes, and when Bramwell was concerned that the other children would think that they were poor, Catherine simply explained, 'So we are'. In later life he recalled, 'She not only patched our clothes, but made us proud of the patches.'

The Christian Mission, as it had now become known, hired various temporary venues. In one, an old wool warehouse in Three Colts Lane, Bethnal Green, youths lit trails of gunpowder that led into the building. On other occasions when the high windows were opened to relieve the oppressive heat from the crowded room, exploding fireworks often rained down on the congregation. This,

however, did not daunt the worshippers, as William recalled, 'Our people got used to this, shouting, "Hallelujah!" when the crackers exploded and the powder flashed.'

From September 1865 the Sunday meetings were held in Professor Orson's Dancing Academy in New Road—these continued until early 1867. The Saturday night dances did not finish until the early hours of Sunday, and William's team of willing workers would often arrive at 4 am bringing in the seating salvaged from the old tent. William would preach in the open air, inviting people to come to the indoor meetings. As they paraded through the streets to the Dancing Academy, they would be joined by others, many of them coming out of their homes and local public houses, attracted by the singing throng.

Thomas Barnardo (1845–1905)

Thomas John Barnardo was the son of a Jewish father and an Irish mother. He became an evangelical Christian in 1862 and joined the Plymouth Brethren. He left Dublin in 1866 to train as a missionary doctor at the London Hospital and at Hudson Taylor's China Inland Mission headquarters in Bow.

While a student, he opened his first Ragged School in Stepney. During this time he met a homeless child, Jim Jarvis, who showed him the extent of child poverty in London's East End. This inspired him to establish his first children's home in 1870. This was followed, in 1876, by the building of a village of seventy cottages to provide homes for girls in Ilford, Essex. By 1878 he had opened fifty orphanages in London. In 1882 he developed a scheme to encourage and equip young people to emigrate to Canada, where there were better employment opportunities.

By the time of his death in 1905, there were more than eight thousand children living in his homes; more than four thousand were boarded out; and eighteen thousand had found new lives in Canada and Australia.

William soon had new converts standing up at his meetings telling the congregation of their conversion to Christ. Leaflets and posters contained billings such as: 'The Milkman who has not watered his milk since he was saved', and 'The converted pigeon flyer'. At the bottom of each handout was the invitation, 'Come—drunk or sober!' One convert, an old gypsy hawker, made such an impression on William that he vowed that he would change his preaching style. He told his son, Bramwell: 'I shall have to burn all those old sermons of mine and go in for the gypsy's.'

In 1866, a young man travelled from Ireland to study medicine at the London Hospital in the Whitechapel Road. Thomas Barnardo joined William in his work in the East End, soon realising, like William, that here was a mission field as vast as any. Moved by the plight of the children on the streets, he went on to found the famous Dr Barnardo's Homes. When he left the work of the Christian Mission, William's parting words were: 'You look after the children and I'll look after the adults. Then together we'll convert the world.'

Rodney Smith joined the work later. A converted gypsy, he was almost illiterate when he began Christian work. After his conversion, Rodney helped his father, Cornelius, and his two uncles as they toured the gypsy sites with the message of salvation. The family soon made

Left: Orsen's Dancing Academy, Whitechapel, scene of the early Christian Mission meetings

apart as Edinburgh and Brighton. William preached wherever he could, renting buildings such as the Apollo and Effingham Theatres, and the skittle alley in Cavell Street. *The Eastern Star,* formerly a beer house in Whitechapel Road, became the first headquarters of the Christian Mission.

In 1868, the Booths moved home to 3, Gore Road, Hackney. This was to be the family home for the next twenty years. On Christmas Day, William had returned from visiting in the area, and seemed disturbed and downcast finding it difficult to enter into the family celebrations. Eventually, he was able to express himself: 'I will never spend a Christmas Day like this again', he said, 'The poor have nothing but the public houses.' Next year, three hundred Christmas dinners were delivered to residents in the area, prepared by Catherine and her faithful cook, Honor Fells, and distributed by Bramwell and a small band of helpers.

By 1870, the Christian Mission needed larger premises and the People's Market, a large building in Whitechapel Road, was purchased for three thousand pounds. Its main hall held 1500 people and its ten smaller rooms and kitchen facilities were ideal for the distribution of soup and other food to the needy. Chunks of bread were sold for a penny to the poor, and were given free to the

contact with William, and at one meeting, without prior warning, he announced that the 'gypsy boy' will speak. Rodney got to his feet and simply told of how he had come to know Jesus Christ as his Saviour. Thus began a seventy-year ministry. 'Gypsy Smith' became a household name throughout the world.

The mission expands

The second half of the 1860s was a period of rapid growth and much movement for the Christian Mission. A number of buildings in the East End were used, while the work was also expanding into suburban areas of London as well as further afield. During this time the Booths conducted missions in various parts of the country as far penniless. It was not long before the simple relief work was supplemented by more long-term aims. An employment bureau was established and alongside this was help for young mothers and pregnant women, and advice and assistance for the many refugees and immigrants who had found their homes in London's poorest borough. By 1872 William had opened five 'Food for the Million' shops, where basic wholesome foods were sold at near cost price. All the time, William never lost sight of the main aim of the Mission, to bring the saving love of Christ to the people whom he felt needed it most.

The two main tragedies of the poor were still identified as alcohol and prostitution. A clinic was set up to help men and women overcome the devastating effects of addiction and women workers befriended prostitutes, some of them still children, and helped them to leave their trade and find worthwhile employment. Those who had a vested interest in the vice and squalor of London's East End intensified their opposition to William and his faithful band. Some of William's workers received savage beatings and many, if not most, had to endure public humiliation. Frequently, they returned to the headquarters covered in the contents of someone's refuse bin!

One particular incident became known as 'The Battle of Sanger's Circus'. A circus tent had been erected on a spot where the Christian missioners usually preached. Seizing the opportunity to speak to the crowds that flocked to the big top, the small band of workers began their meeting. As they sang they were pelted with clods of earth and grass by the circus employees. This was soon followed by the emergence of a brass band, that made 'a hideous noise.' As the preacher began to speak, two men emerged from the

Above: *The London Hospital, Whitechapel Road where Barnardo began his medical training*

Above: Gore Road, Hackney. Number three was the Booth's family home for twenty years

tent and stood in front of him. One banged on a bass drum, while the other crashed a large pair of cymbals. This did not deter the preacher who continued to urge men and women to come to Christ. An elephant and two dromedaries were then led into the crowd of onlookers causing panic. It was a near miracle that no one was injured or killed.

The early 1870s brought sickness and sadness to the Booth household. In 1870, William was ill again, and spent three months recuperating. In the same year Catherine's mother, who had been such a great help in the early days of the work, died of breast cancer. During the latter half of the decade the most important part of William's work would be fulfilled. It was preceded by the arrival of two men who rallied to the cause.

George Scott Railton joined the Christian Mission in March 1873. Somewhat eccentric, he was to add an intellectual dimension to the Mission's leadership that had previously been lacking. Born in 1849, the son of Methodist missionaries, he had spent much of his life in seeking the right place in which to serve his Saviour. Railton was converted to Christ at the age of ten. On leaving school he obtained a post with an Anglo-Spanish merchant but it was not long before he was engaged in full-time Christian service—as a missioner to Spanish seamen in London Docks—and then he set off for Morocco. He soon ran out of money and, with the help of the British Consul, returned to England by working his passage as a ship's steward. Within a year he had settled in Middlesborough as a Methodist evangelist. On reading William's pamphlet, *How to reach the masses with the gospel*, Railton felt that this was the work that God had called him to. Without any preparation or warning, he hastily left for London and presented himself on the Booth's

Above: George Scott Railton (left) and Elijah Cadnam, influential figures in the formation of The Salvation Army

doorstep in Gore Road, Hackney. Railton remained a member of the household for eleven years and, as William's secretary and later the first Commissioner, became a driving force within the Salvation Army until his death in 1913.

Elijah Cadman joined the Mission in 1876. As a child of six he became one of the thousands of boys who were employed by chimney sweeps in the dangerous and unhealthy occupation of clearing the thick crusts of soot from inside the chimneys. Cadman grew into a tough young man. He moved to nearby Rugby where he joined with a local gang. By this time he was virtually an alcoholic and using his skill with his fists, he opened a boxing booth at a local public house. His conversion was as clear cut and dramatic as his preaching would later become. In December 1861, he and a friend were watching a public hanging outside Warwick Prison. As the body dropped and the rope did its work, Cadman's friend remarked, 'That's where you will come to, Elijah, one day.' True to character, Elijah went home, smashed his boxing booth and swore that he would no longer smoke or drink alcohol. Whereas Railton was an intellectual, Cadman was a man of action. He became a Methodist preacher, billing himself as, 'The Saved Sweep from Rugby'. It was not long before he heard of William Booth's work in London and was attracted to join the Christian Mission. He was a gifted evangelist who, although often outrageous, could attract and keep the attention of people who would otherwise be indifferent to the claims of Christ. It was a typically impulsive outrageous action by Cadman that signalled the beginning of The Salvation Army.

THE WHITECHAPEL WALK

1 THE 'BLIND BEGGAR'
2 BUST OF WILLIAM BOOTH
3 STATUE OF WILLIAM BOOTH
4 SITE OF 'THE EASTERN STAR'
5 SITE OF SKITTLE ALLEY
6 DANCING ACADEMY

7 SITE OF 102 CHRISTIAN STREET—WHERE WOMEN'S HOSTELS BEGAN
8 SITE OF EBENEEZER HALL
9 WHITECHAPEL BELL FOUNDRY

10 SITE OF PEOPLE'S MISSION
11 SITE OF EFFINGHAM THEATRE
12 SITE OF PAVILION THEATRE
13 SITE OF SUNDIAL TENT

TRAVEL INFORMATION

The Congestion Charge and difficulty with parking make it advisable to use public transport when travelling in Central London.

The Whitechapel Walk

This walk takes you to some of the places associated with the life and work of William Booth during the early days of the Christian Mission (founded 1865). There is little left of the original buildings, but as you visit the sites it is not difficult to imagine what it was like in William Booth's day. Allow approximately 2 hrs for the walk. We begin at:

Whitechapel Station which is situated in the Whitechapel Market. On market days, the streets are very crowded and busy. It is good to come at such times as, although the culture is very different now, it gives us a flavour of this part of London during Booth's day.

By public transport: Enquiries: 020 7222 1234. Underground: Whitechapel (District Line and Hammersmith and City lines). Rail: East London Line, (from New

Cross and Wapping). Bus service: 25 from Oxford Circus; 106 from Finsbury Park; 253 from Euston Station. The London Hospital, which is almost directly opposite is a good focal point.

On leaving the station, turn left along Whitechapel Road to the busy junction with Cambridge Heath Road. On the left hand corner is *The Blind Beggar*.

The Blind Beggar Public House

Outside this public house, in June 1865, William Booth 'found his destiny'. The Whitechapel Road was teeming with people who had little hope. Their poverty was obvious. There were many 'gin palaces' that sold cheap liquor. It seemed to William that here, concentrated in this one street in London, were all the causes and effects of the sin and degradation that had driven him to become a preacher of the gospel. Outside *The Blind Beggar* there was a small group of Christians trying to attract the attention of the passing crowds. William was invited to preach. As the tall, bearded, young evangelist looked around at the people who had stopped to listen; his heart went

Above: *Erected in 1950, the statue of William Booth at Mile End Road*

out to them. He simply spoke of the saving power of Jesus Christ. The effect was electric—many wanted to know more. The Christians present were so impressed; they asked William to take charge of a tent mission they were holding nearby. From this spot William launched a mission that would encompass the whole world!

The original frontage of

The Blind Beggar was replaced in 1894, and in recent years the adjoining building has been demolished and is now a beer garden.

Cross the Cambridge Heath Road to the junction with Mile End Road. On the corner, at the beginning of a narrow grassed avenue of trees that stretched up the Mile End Road, we find the bust of William Booth.

The bust of William Booth

This was unveiled in 1927 and faces the busy road. This is the beginning of what is left of the original Mile End Waste, where William often used to preach the gospel.

Continuing east, through the tree-lined avenue, along the Mile End Road, we come to The statue of William Booth.

The Statue of William Booth

This was erected in 1950 to commemorate the 150th anniversary of his birth (10 April 1829). This was the site of *The Vine* public house. Adjacent is the Methodist Mission, and some alms-houses, that would have been there in William's day. Not far from this statue is a bust of King Edward VII, erected in 1911, a year before William died.

Return to *The Blind Beggar* and cross to the opposite side of the Whitechapel Road.

A little way along, on the left is 220 Whitechapel Road.

Above: The Eastern Star, Whitechapel, acquired by Booth in 1867

220 Whitechapel Road

Now an electronics shop, this is the site of *The Eastern Star,* a run down public house that William acquired in 1867 and turned into the Christian Mission's first Headquarters. The facade of no. 222 gives us an idea of what the original building looked like.

Continue down Whitechapel Road and turn left into Cavell Street. On the right, near the corner of Cavell Street and Raven Row is the site of the Skittle Alley.

The Skittle Alley

On this site, that is now a parking area for Post Office vans, stood the Alexandra Hall, a covered skittle alley, where William used to preach on Sunday mornings and afternoons in 1867 and 1870.

Continue along Cavell Street to Ford Square. Here is a good example of Victorian London. At the end of the Square turn right into Varden Street. At the end of Varden Street turn left and cross New Road to the Dancing Academy.

The Dancing Academy

After the tent on the disused Quaker Burial ground had blown down, William moved his operations into Professor Orson's Dancing Academy. The blue plaque on the building dates it as Sunday 3 September 1865. In the early hours of a Sunday morning, after the Saturday night dances had finished, William and his helpers would get busy cleaning and preparing the place for the Sunday services. This continued until February 1867.

Continue along New Road to the busy Commercial Road. Cross and turn right. The third turning on the left is Christian Street.

102 Christian Street

It was at this site that the, now world famous, Salvation Army rescue work unofficially began. One evening in 1881, after praying with a girl at one of their meetings, Sergeant Elizabeth Cottrill discovered that the girl lived in a notorious local brothel. Elizabeth took her home to Christian Street. A Knitwear company now occupies the building.

Return to and cross Commercial Road. Turn right and then left into Parfett Street. Continue down the pedestrian area and past the junction with Fordham Street. At the end of Parfett Street, turn left into Fieldgate Street. Between Settles Street and Greenfield Road is a clothing factory. This is the site of The Ebenezer Hall.

The Ebenezer Hall

This became the Christian Mission meeting place in 1870. In 1880, two years after the Salvation Army was founded, *The War Cry* was printed and distributed from here. Opposite is the rear entrance of the East London Mosque, which almost overshadows an adjacent synagogue.

Continue to the end of Fieldgate Street to the Whitechapel Road. At the end of Fieldgate Street is the Whitechapel Bell Foundry. Built in 1670, William would have been familiar with this building. It was here that many of the great bells were cast, including: The Liberty Bell; the Great Westminster Bell (Big Ben); the Cathedral bells of Montreal, Lincoln, St Paul's, and Liverpool; and the bells of Westminster Abbey. Tours of the foundry can be made on Saturday mornings. An appointment has to be made first. ☎ 020 7247 2599. Fax: 020 7375 1979.

Email:bells@whitechapelbellfoundry.co.uk

Turn left into Whitechapel Road. Nos. 22–22 is the site of: The People's Mission Hall.

The People's Mission Hall

This site, originally the People's Market, was purchased by the Christian Mission in 1870. Its main hall held up to 1500 people. It had 10 smaller rooms and an adjoining soup and coffee house. This Mission moved its headquarters here from 220 Whitechapel Road, and it remained so until 1881 when the Salvation Army set up its headquarters in Queen Victoria Street. By 1893 it had became the headquarters of the Men's Social Work, including a men's hostel.

Cross Whitechapel Road. Turn right. Across the road lies the imposing front of the East London Mosque. A little way along is a Citroen Garage and Showroom. This is the site of:

The Effingham Theatre

As the work of the Christian Mission rapidly expanded, this building was also used as a preaching station between 1867 and 1870.

Continue along

Above: Site of Quaker Burial ground Vallence Road

Whitechapel Road. On the left, next to a Drama School, is a vacant site. On here stood no. 193:

The Pavilion Theatre

The Christian Mission used this for a brief period when the Effingham Theatre was being rebuilt.

Turn left into Vallence Road. On the right, is Vallence Road Gardens, flanked by a housing estate. In the Gardens there is a drinking fountain, and the remains of a sundial that marks the place of The Tent.

The Tent

This is the site of the disused Quaker Burial ground where William, after preaching for the first time outside *The Blind Beggar* conducted the first tent missions of his campaign. The date was Sunday 2 July 1865. In the surrounding streets stood the Hanbury Street Rescue Home (1884), and the Women's Shelter (1898).

Return to Whitechapel Road and turn left. Continue to Whitechapel Station where our walk ends.

Those who wish to visit William Booth's grave can do so from here. There are two alternative routes:

1. Take the Hammersmith and City line from Whitechapel to Liverpool Street. Change over to the BR system to Stoke Newington.

2. Continue past Whitechapel Station and turn left into Brady Street. At the end of Brady Street, bear right into Three Colts Lane. Bethnal Green Station is on the right. Take a train to Stoke Newington.

Directions to the cemetery and a description of the walk are to be found in **The Abney Park Cemetery Walk on page 117.**

Ragged School Museum

46–48 Copperfield Road, Bow, London, E3 4RR
☎ 020 8980 6405
Open on Wednesdays and Thursdays 1000–1700 hrs
First Sunday of the month 1400–1700 hrs
Admission free—donations appreciated.

Ragged Schools were started in London in the late 1830s to teach poor children about the Bible and to read and write.

❼ Blood and Fire

On an early May morning in 1878, in William Booth's bedroom, the Salvation Army was born—with William as its first General. Within two years it had raised its flag in the United States. Before long its uniforms were seen and its bands were heard on every continent

As the work of the Mission progressed, it was evident that its committee structure, inherited from Methodism, was not working. Railton in particular wanted William to take sole control of the movement. It had become increasingly evident that they were now thinking in terms of an army. There was a growing use of military jargon in describing the work and its successes. This came to a head when in November 1877 Elijah Cadman declared 'war' on Whitby, a fishing town on the north-east coast of England. Cadman and Railton had, from the outset, considered themselves soldiers in God's army. Cadman, describing himself as 'Captain', announced the mission's arrival with the poster: 'War! War! 200 men and women wanted at once to join the Hallelujah Army!' The Whitby 'siege' lasted six months and was a great success. Cadman's tactics and terminology repelled the respectable residents and local clergy, but the poorer classes flocked to the meetings and over three thousand conversions were recorded. When William visited the town, a poster was produced billing him as the 'General of the

Above: The familiar Salvation Army Crest contains powerful symbolism including the sun's rays which represent Christ as the Light of the World

Facing page: In the shadow of St Paul's. The Salvation Army Headquarters at 101 Queen Victoria Street, now being rebuilt

Hallelujah Army'. Hiding the poster in his house, Cadman hoped that during William's visit it would go unnoticed. His leader, however, spotted it and far from disapproving, commended Cadman on his ingenuity. The die was now cast for the future of the Mission.

The founding of The Salvation Army

During May 1878, William worked on the annual report of the Christian Mission. Early one morning he summoned Bramwell and Railton to his bedroom to read through the proofs. The preliminary statement referred to the Christian Mission as a Volunteer Army. Bramwell strongly objected. He was not a *volunteer*, for he was compelled by God to do what he had to do. His father and Railton heartily agreed, and, taking up his pen,

***Above:** Catherine Booth seen in the distinctive uniform of The Salvation Army*

William crossed out the word *Volunteer* and replaced it with *Salvation*. The Christian Mission had a new name and a new direction. At the Mission's congress in August, its constitution was scrapped and by the end of the year William ceased to be known as Reverend and took total command as the General.

A flurry of activity followed. The mission stations, dotted throughout the country, were now called 'Corps'. A crest was designed, to be worn by the Salvationists as a mark of identification. The sun's rays represented Christ as the Light of the World; the cross occupied a central place and two swords depicted the Bible, the Word of God; the letter 'S' stood for salvation; a crown topped the crest, showing the Salvationists' belief that those who remained faithful would receive the crown of eternal life. The motto, 'Blood and Fire'—declared the source of the Salvationists' power: the blood of Christ that cleansed the repentant sinner—and the fire of the Holy Spirit that enabled him to live in a relationship with God. A flag was created based upon the crest, with red, yellow and blue colours representing the blood of Christ, the baptism of the Holy Spirit, and holiness. Military terminology that had evolved during the life of the Christian Mission was now employed in almost every area of Salvation Army life: prayer became *knee drill*; speeches became *bombshells*; and the giving of an offering was called *firing a cartridge*.

Above: *The band from Stotfold Corps in Bedfordshire. Note the variety of dress and instruments in this early Salvation Army Band*

Uniforms and bands

During the early weeks and months of the Army, Salvationists identified themselves as best they could. Some wore the brass letter 'S' in their lapels; others wore red and blue armbands. The Army crest was worn on stovepipe hats, and some even cut the title from *The War Cry*—the name given to the Army's newspaper—and tucked it into the hatband. It took almost two years to produce a standard uniform that could be purchased by Salvation Army officers. A navy blue serge uniform was introduced for both men and women. Men wore a high necked tunic over a red jersey. Their headgear was a military cap with a red band, and the words *The Salvation Army* depicted in gold.

Women wore long navy skirts, high-necked tunics with white lace-edged collars. Catherine and her daughter Kate designed a straw bonnet with a red band and large ribbons. It was smart, functional and gave the women some protection from missiles. This became known as the 'Hallelujah Bonnet' and remained in use for almost one hundred years.

Music had always played a prominent part in William's ministry. From the early days in Whitechapel, the fiddle, tin whistle, concertina, or any instrument available had accompanied the songs. The make up of each band was determined by the availability of instruments and musicians. Many were a hotchpotch of leaky old brass instruments, drums, cymbals, banjos and anything that sounded vaguely musical! From the early days, William had insisted on catchy tunes that the unchurched would be able to pick up easily. It was not long before secular, often bawdy and profane, music hall ditties were adapted with Christian lyrics. Like many Christians, before and since, William was uneasy about this. He was always willing to use all means to bring the people to faith in Christ, but he was unhappy about the source of some of the songs he was beginning to hear from his troops: 'Here's to good old whiskey' became, 'Storm the forts of darkness, bring them down'. The blending of the sacred with the secular was always a problem. However, William's mind was made up on a visit to Worcester in 1882. George 'Sailor' Fielder, the Commanding officer was asked to sing, 'Bless His name, He set me free.' William was greatly moved by the song. After the meeting, he remarked, 'That was a fine song. What tune was it?' and was surprised to hear from a disapproving fellow officer: 'That's "Champagne Charlie is my name"'. Turning to Bramwell, William commented, 'Why should the devil have all the best tunes?'

A few months later, at one of the Army's conventions, Gypsy Smith sang, 'O the blood of Jesus cleanses white as snow' to the tune, 'I traced her little footprints in the snow'. William was there, nodding his approval.

The 'Hallelujah Lasses'

The Hallelujah Lasses made the most noticeable impact. These were the women officers whom William sent throughout the country. Some, like Eliza Haynes, became national figures. 'Happy Eliza' caused a stir wherever she went. During her time in her native Sheffield, she paraded through the streets, with streamers floating from her unbraided hair, singing, 'Shout aloud Salvation boys', to the tune 'Marching to Georgia.' Eliza became so popular that music hall ditties were written about her, and even dolls and sweets were named after her.

In 1879 seventeen-year-old Kate Shepherd was sent to open the Army's work in the Rhondda Valley in Wales. When Catherine arrived at the end of the year to present the Salvation Army flag to the corps, an estimated fifteen hundred people were waiting to greet

Above: 'Happy' Eliza Haynes—pictured violin in hand—one of the young women officers who caused a sensation as they took the Gospel to the people

Above: The People's Mission, Whitechapel, 1870s

her. It is said that Kate received six offers of marriage during her first six weeks of preaching—two from ordained ministers!

It was in Tyneside that the impact of young women missioners was exemplified. Here they were first called the 'Hallelujah Lasses.' William had sent six young women to Gateshead where they took the town by storm. By the time he and Catherine arrived, over nine thousand people had attended meetings and there were one hundred and forty converts, many of them known to the local police.

Converts from the lowest depths of society were put to work, many of them becoming serving officers in the Army. Most of them were unlearned and some were illiterate. Former prostitutes, alcoholics, and hardened criminals swelled the ranks of William's troops—their billing unashamedly telling the world where they had come from. Billy Herdman: 'The drunken escapologist', George Fox: 'The converted clown', Happy Hannah: 'The reformed smoker', and many more, urged men and women from their own class to come to Christ.

As the work grew, more premises were needed to accommodate and train the influx of new recruits. The Booths moved from Gore Road to Clapton Common, enabling the house to be used for the accommodation and training of thirty women. A men's training establishment was set up in

Devonshire House, in Mare Street, Hackney. It was not until 1929 that the Salvation Army would open the international William Booth Training College in Camberwell, South London. In 1880, the Army moved its headquarters to 101, Queen Victoria Street, not far from St Paul's Cathedral.

Across the Atlantic

In the same year a new horizon opened for Booth. Railton urged the General to send him and seven 'Hallelujah Lasses' to the United States of America. In 1878, Amos Shirley—a Salvationist—had emigrated to Philadelphia to make a new life for himself and his family. His wife Annie, and daughter Eliza had remained in England until sent for. Annie had been converted at a Salvation Army meeting in Coventry and at the age of seventeen had been made a lieutenant. When Amos had established himself in employment, he sent for his wife and daughter. Eliza, who by now was doing a great work for the Army in England, sought the General's permission to go to America and begin working there. William reluctantly agreed and the Shirley family was reunited.

While Amos continued to support his family through his work in a silk factory, the two women began to work on the streets of the city. They turned a disused factory into a meeting place and began to preach the gospel. They must have felt that they were back home in England when they were pelted with eggs and rotten vegetables as they toured the streets inviting the poor and homeless to their meetings. The turning point came when some youths set light to a barrel of tar on a piece of wasteland where the Shirleys were holding an open-air meeting. As the local fire brigade doused the flames, a ragged figure approached Amos– 'Is it true what you say? Will your God take the devil's leavings and make something out of them? I'll give him a chance.' Amos was able to tell him that it was true, and this man became the first Salvation Army convert in the United States.

William eventually agreed that Railton should go to America and, on 14 February 1880, he and seven women officers set sail, docking in New York three weeks later. Two of the women were sent to help the Shirleys in Philadelphia, while

Above: William Booth Training College, Denmark Hill, Camberwell, constructed in 1929. Behind the vast, austere frontage lies a thriving international community

Above: During the 1880s, The Salvation Army was established as a worldwide organisation, based on the 'soup, soap and salvation' principle which began in London

Railton and the others 'declared war' on New York. The contrast between wealth and poverty in the city was stark. Theatres, brothels and gambling dens abounded, while in the poorer downtown areas poverty was rampant. Hardened by their work in the East End of London, Railton and his troops were still visibly shocked by what awaited them in the city's East Side. The population density was nearly three thousand per square mile, and ten thousand homeless children littered the streets, mixing with the drunks that slept on the sidewalks. A lesser man than Railton may have been overwhelmed by the prospect of bringing the gospel to such a place. But he was never off duty, even wearing a brass 'S' on his nightshirt to remind him of the fact!

The first public meeting was held in Harry Hill's Variety Theatre, where Railton had persuaded the owner to let him preach to the theatre audience. The evening was not a rousing success, and soon the ardent Salvationist was removed from the stage. Railton, however, was convinced that God was at work, and this became evident when he returned to Baxter Street. James

Kemp had not attended the meeting, but on hearing of what had taken place, he was soon knocking on Railton's door. Nicknamed 'Ash Barrel Jimmy' because he had once tumbled into an ash barrel and had to be prised out, Kemp was a drunken old reprobate. 'Is it true that God could save sinners like me?' he enquired. 'Yes, it is true', Railton replied. Converted to Christ, James Kemp became a loyal Salvationist, rising to the rank of Captain by the time of his death in Boston in 1895. As in London and Philadelphia, the floodgates were now open for the expansion of the work in New York.

Christianity with its sleeves rolled up

The 1880s saw the Salvation Army established as a worldwide organisation. By 1887, Britain had a thousand corps, and there were similar units on every continent, with William Booth visiting many of its outposts. Soon the principle of 'soup, soap and salvation' was operating from Argentina to Australia and from Iceland to Zululand! In 1882, the first Prison-Gate Home was opened for the rehabilitation of released prisoners. Two years later, a Rescue Home was opened in Hanbury Street for prostitutes seeking to break the vice-like grip of their pimps. In 1887, a Slum Settlement was opened. The hungry were not forgotten and in Limehouse, not far from Whitechapel, the first Food Depot was established.

As the Army grew, so did its influence and status. Beneath the proud and pious veneer of Victorian Society, there was a corrupt and degenerate underworld inhabited by its helpless victims. In the middle of the decade the Army became involved in an issue that brought it to the forefront of Britain's

Above: A Salvation Army officer in a Scottish alcohol detox unit talking with a client

Above: *Where there's brass: since its early beginnings, the familiar brass instruments have become a hallmark of The Salvation Army*

national consciousness. Used to waging war on publicans and pimps, the Salvationists were about to launch their attack on some of the pillars of society.

Early one February morning in 1885, Annie Swan, a seventeen-year-old from Shoreham in Sussex was found huddled on the doorstep of the Army's Headquarters in Queen Victoria Street. She had come to London in answer to an advertisement for domestic staff, only to find that she had been duped into the savage clutches of a brothel keeper in Pimlico. Realising her plight she had locked herself in the kitchen and managed to escape before dawn. Alone in London, and knowing of the Army and its work, she turned to the only ones she felt could help her. Annie was taken to Bramwell's office and spilled out her story to the Chief of Staff. He was visibly shocked when she told him of girls much younger than her who were held as virtual slaves to satisfy the lusts of the rich clientele. From its inception the Salvation Army had dealt with prostitution—this matter, however, was different—it amounted to child slavery! Bramwell's wife, Florence, who daily faced the task of rescuing and rehabilitating the street girls, verified Annie's story. Bramwell was filled with holy indignation. More needed to be learned of this foul trade, but how?

The answer came in the person of William T. Stead, a crusading journalist and the editor of the influential *Pall Mall Gazette*, who arranged a meeting and agreed to investigate the matter. Rebecca Jarrett, who was a converted brothel keeper, verified the extent of the trade. Both men chilled when Jarrett told them of young girls, their virginity verified by a midwife, being drugged and transported in coffins, to be sold to wealthy clients. The legal age of consent was thirteen years, and with few of the girls able to produce birth certificates, this

Stead to the dark world of London's prostitution and, posing as a rich client, Stead purchased thirteen year old Eliza Armstrong from her mother for five pounds. The frightened child was taken through the whole process experienced by thousands of other unfortunate children. Great pains were taken to verify that no sexual molestation of the child took place. His account caused a furore. He was accused of sensationalizing the issue in order to sell his paper; some even accused him of publishing pornography. He and five others were arrested and put on trial for his actions. Bramwell escaped prosecution. Stead was jailed for three months. However, he had made his point, and, as a result of the publicity, Parliament passed the *Criminal Amendment Act*, which raised the age of consent from thirteen to sixteen.

In the wake of the success of the Eliza Armstrong case, the Army set about the task of rescuing prostitutes from streets and brothels throughout the world. Within five years the Army had established thirteen homes in the United Kingdom.

But now some shattering news had reached the Booth household.

became virtually impossible to prove. To make matters worse, many of the men involved were influential, some were even Members of Parliament.

Stead set out to investigate and publish details of this foul trade. Enlisting Bramwell's help, he laid out a plan that would blow the lid off the trade once and for all. They would prove how easy it was to purchase a child by procuring one for themselves! Rebecca Jarrett was reluctantly recruited, as she had access to, and knowledge of, the underworld of London's vice. Realising the dangers of what they were about to do, they informed prominent Christian leaders of their plan. Jarrett introduced

The Congestion Charge and difficulty with parking make it advisable to use public transport when travelling in Central London.

Above: The Crystal Palace much used by The Salvation Army during Booth's time

Salvation Army International Heritage Centre

The William Booth Training College
Denmark Hill, London, SE5 8BQ
☎ 020 7332 0101/ 020 7332 8056
e-mail: heritage@salvationarmy.org
website: www.salvationarmy.org/history

By public transport:
Rail: Denmark Hill Station is directly opposite. Trains run from Victoria, Blackfriars and London Bridge. Bus service—42, 68, 176, 185, 468.
Enquiries:
☎ 020 7222 1234

Regent Hall

275 Oxford Street, London, WC1
☎ 020 7629 5424
Regent hall is situated between Regent Street and New Bond Street. The Salvation Army began using the building— formerly a skating rink— in 1882. William Booth spoke there many times. It is still a focal point of Salvation Army work, with a world famous band and songsters. There are lunchtime concerts at 1300 hrs every Friday (admission free).
By car: parking on meters 0830—1830 hrs Mon-Sat. car park in Cavendish Square (behind British Home Stores)
By public transport:
Underground—Oxford Circus (Central, Victoria and Bakerloo lines) or Bond Street (Central and Jubilee lines). Bus service—6, 7, 8, 10, 13, 15, 16, 25, 73, 84, 94, 98, 135, 137, 137a, 176

The Crystal Palace

London, SE19
The Salvation Army used this great glass exhibition centre for meetings during William Booth's time. On the twenty-fifth anniversary of its founding, in 1890, William Booth addressed a large congregation. The dying Catherine Booth's last letter was also read to them. It was in this building that CH Spurgeon famously preached at a Fast Day Service in 1857. The building was destroyed by fire in 1936. The park remains, with some of the original features still visible. The lake is surrounded by statues of prehistoric animals that were there in Booth's day. There is a small museum in Anerley Hill that is open on Sundays. Nearby is the National Sports Centre which caters for over 100 indoor and outdoor sporting activities. For details:
☎ 020 8778 0131. email: info@crystalpalace.co.uk
By car: Take the South Circular (A205) turn right at junction with Croxted Road (A2199). Continue on A2199 to Crystal Palace Parade. Parking in side streets.
By public transport:
Rail—Crystal Palace. Bus services—2, 3, 63, 122, 202, 227, 249, 322, 358, 410, 417, 450

8 In darkest England and the way out

William Booth launched his great social plan, *In Darkest England and the Way Out*. Now, as an honoured international figure, he embarked on exhausting motor tours of Britain and visited Salvation Army companies across the world. Failing health did not daunt him until the General, frail and blind, was finally promoted to glory

On 21 February 1888, William waited nervously for his wife to return home to Hadley Wood from a visit to central London. He was anxious to see Catherine and hear the news of her visit. As the carriage pulled into the drive, he rushed out to meet it.

Sometime in 1887, Catherine had noticed a small lump in her left breast. She had ignored it until persuaded by Bramwell to get a medical examination. Her journey had been to the Harley Street consulting rooms of the eminent surgeon, Sir James Paget. William saw from his wife's tear stained cheeks that the news was not good. He ushered her into the drawing room and waited for an explanation. He was stunned by the news. Catherine had a malignant tumour and Sir John recommended immediate surgery. During the journey home, Catherine had tried to come to terms with the news that she had just heard. She had fallen to her knees in the carriage and cast herself upon the mercy and loving care of her Saviour. Catherine

Above: 'Rookstone,' the Booths' home in Hadley Wood, Hertfordshire

thought back to the time when she had nursed her dying mother through the same disease. One thing was sure in her mind—her daughters would not have to look after her! She was also pondering the question of surgery. Catherine had been blunt with Paget: 'How long will I live if I do not have the operation?' The surgeon's reply was a death sentence: 'Approximately two years.' William tried to take in all that his wife was telling him. To make matters worse, he was due to leave her in a few hours for Holland to conduct meetings in Amsterdam. His mind was in turmoil. How could he leave his wife now?

Catherine rose from her seat and knelt beside her husband: 'Do you know what was my first thought?' she sobbed, 'That I should not be here to nurse you during your last hour.' William described his feelings at that moment: 'I was stunned. I felt as if the whole world were coming to a standstill. . . I could only kneel with her and try to pray.' William had already decided that he would not go to Holland but Catherine would have none of it and insisted that he should fulfil his commitment. As ever, guided by his wife's deep sense of duty, he agreed. Stopping briefly in London to inform Bramwell of the news, he made his way to Amsterdam.

After two sessions of the conference, he decided that he must return to England. Leaving others to continue the meetings, he made his way back across the English Channel. William was to

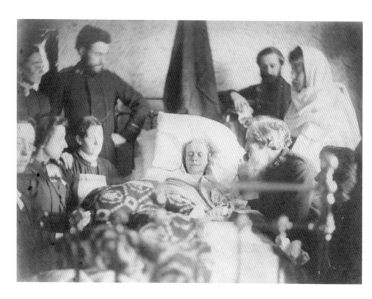

Above: Deathbed scene. Surrounded by William and her family, the dying Catherine Booth lies beneath the flag of The Salvation Army

Above: The City Temple, London where Catherine Booth preached her final sermon in June 1888

destroying the lives of millions! The Booths had long battled against the social evils that had driven the poor into lives of sin and vice. Until now, the battlefield had been confined to the slum areas of the world. William was working on a project that would take the fight into the world arena and thrust him prominently into the public eye.

In Darkest England

On 1 December 1887, William had been returning from a speaking engagement. Just after midnight, as his carriage made its way across London Bridge, he noticed scores of people huddled together in every nook and cranny that afforded shelter from the cold wind. His life's work had familiarised him with poverty, but he had not until now realised its extent. After angrily confronting Bramwell on the matter, he ordered Salvation Army officers to investigate the extent of the homelessness and report back to him. As document after document piled up on his desk he realised that here was a social cancer that had to be fought and eradicated. With the help of William Stead, he began work on *In Darkest England and the Way Out*.

In Victorian England, the Poor Law governed the way in which society dealt with those who could not support themselves. It was the state's responsibility to provide food and shelter for those who could not find employment, but the system was so structured as to make it virtually impossible for thousands to comply with the regulations. William was

face two years of intense struggle in forwarding the work of the Salvation Army, and comforting his dying wife. This was the most painful experience of his life: 'To go home was anguish. To be away was worse. Life became a burden, almost too heavy to be borne, until God in a very definite manner visited me in a measure, and comforted my heart.'

As he watched his wife battle against cancer, William engaged in his own fight against another malignant disease that was determined that he would bring this to the public notice and that the Salvation Army would focus its attention and resources in setting up its own programme of reform. William laboured long and hard at his desk, frequently seeking advice and encouragement from Catherine. He would often hear the cries of pain coming from her room as the nurses dressed her suppurating wound.

Catherine preached her last sermon at the City Temple in London, on 1 June 1888. She was rarely seen in public after this. In August 1889, the Booths set up home in Clacton-on-Sea, Essex. It was felt that the sea air might have a beneficial effect on Catherine's health. Periods where death seemed imminent were followed by times of remission, when she was able to receive visitors and dictate letters. Appropriately, her last letter on 'self-denial' was published in *The War Cry* on the day of her death!

By September 1890, William and Stead at last finished the 140,000 word manuscript of *In Darkest England and the Way Out*. Stead was convinced that it would 'echo round the world'. In his exuberance he remarked, 'I rejoice with an exceeding great joy.' 'And I', whispered Catherine, 'and I most of all. Thank God. Thank God.'

Above: Clapton Congress Hall, where, over a period of five days in October 1890, almost fifty thousand people filed past to pay their final tributes to Catherine Booth

Promoted to glory

On Saturday afternoon, 4 October 1890, with her family around her bedside, the Mother of the Salvation Army was promoted to glory. As William bent to kiss his beloved goodbye, her arms went round his neck, 'Pa', she gasped, and sank back on the pillow. The body of Catherine Booth was taken to the Clapton Congress Hall, where, over a period of five days, almost fifty thousand people filed past to pay their final tributes.

On 13 October, thirty six thousand people crammed into the Olympia Grand Hall, in West London, for the funeral service. The coffin was taken in procession through the streets of London to Abney Park Cemetery. Led by a parade of three thousand Salvation Army officers, William stood upright in his carriage, acknowledging the salutes of the

Above: Following the funeral service at Olympia's Grand Hall, West London (attended by 36,000) the committal of Catherine Booth took place at Abney Park Cemetery on 13 October 1890

many thousands who had gathered on the streets. Railton conducted the graveside committal, but before Catherine's coffin was lowered into its final resting-place, William rose to speak: 'My comrades, I am going to meet her again. I have never turned from her these forty years for any journeyings on my mission of mercy but I have longed to get back, and have counted the weeks, days, and hours which should take me again to her side. When she has gone away from me it has been just the same. And now she has gone away for the last time … My work plainly is to fill up the weeks, the days, and the hours, and cheer my poor heart as I go along with the thought that, when I have served my Christ and my generation according to the will of God—which I vow this afternoon I will, to my last drop of blood— then I trust that she will bid me welcome to the skies, as He bade her. God bless you all. Amen.'

The work continues

It was not long before the grieving General had launched himself back into the fight. In October 1890 *In Darkest England and the Way Out* was published. Within a year it had sold two hundred thousand copies. In it, William outlined his plan to reform society. A major theme was what William termed, 'The Cab Horse Charter'. The cab horse, William Booth argued, was treated better than millions of the poorest people. His plan captured the imagination of the public and the support of a number of prominent

Above and below: One pioneering initiative was the purchase of a farm, in Hadleigh, Essex, to enable men who had not worked for years to regain their self-respect and be trained for future employment

businessmen. An employment bureau was set up to find people work. A farm, in Hadleigh, Essex, was purchased to enable men who had not worked for years to regain their self-respect and be trained for future employment. Other projects included: a missing persons bureau; a 'poor man's bank' that gave loans so that men could purchase the tools of their trade; and hostels providing clean, dry, accommodation. By the turn of the 19th century, The Salvation Army had served twenty seven million cheap meals, lodged eleven million homeless people, traced eighteen thousand missing persons and found jobs for nine thousand unemployed. The effect of *In Darkest England and the Way Out* continued long after William's death. In 1948, it became the blueprint for the establishment of Britain's Welfare State scheme. The dream that began in the 'Bottoms' in Nottingham was now becoming a reality on a worldwide scale!

Another project dear to William's heart was the opening of a Salvation Army match factory. It was discovered that a mother and two children under nine years of age were working 16 hours a day in appalling conditions for as little as two shillings a week. To make

*With fine views over the nearby country parks, Hadleigh Farm and training centre is well worth a visit. **By car:** From the M25 take the A13 London Road to Hadleigh. Castle Lane is opposite the Waggon and Horses. ☎ 01702 552963*

matters worse, they were using yellow phosphorus—a dangerous substance that resulted in many contracting necrosis or 'phossy jaw' a painful and often fatal disease. William decided to act. In 1891, the Salvation Army opened their own factory producing matches from the much safer red phosphorus. The matches called 'Lights in Darkest England', were produced in improved working conditions with better pay and facilities for the workers.

World travel

Throughout the 1890s the Salvation Army was establishing its work throughout the world. William too was becoming an international figure. In 1891 he made his first visits to South Africa, Australia, and New Zealand, visiting India on the way home. During the early 1900s William was treated like a world statesman, being received by King Haakon of Norway, King Gustav of Sweden, and the Emperor of

Japan. In 1905 he visited the Holy Land and preached at the Garden Tomb. As he approached the Garden of Gethsemene, William Booth knelt to kiss a leper's hand. He made frequent visits to the USA, having a particular affinity with the people there. In 1903 President Roosevelt received him, and two years later William was invited to lead the Senate in prayer.

Ever an innovator, he saw the potential of the increasingly popular motor car, and in 1904 began the first of seven motor campaigns throughout Britain. Throughout his own nation William was now being feted as one of the great figures of the age. In 1905 he was given the freedom of the city of his birth— Nottingham—and in the same year London honoured him in similar fashion. The University of Oxford awarded him an honorary Doctorate of Civil Law in 1907. On 24 June 1904, William Booth was invited to Buckingham Palace to meet King Edward VII. William was astonished when the King asked him for his autograph! Taking the pen in his hand he wrote, 'Some men's ambition is art. Some men's ambition is fame. Some men's ambition is gold. My ambition is the souls of men.'

'I've fought the fight'

By the time William made his last visit to the USA in 1907 his eyesight was beginning to fail. In 1908 an operation to remove a cataract from his right eye was performed. It was partially successful, but by 1910 he had became totally blind in that eye with only a little sight in the other. This did not daunt William in his mission. He continued to travel around Europe, fulfilling preaching engagements and surveying the work of The Salvation Army. He also embarked on his seventh motor tour of Britain. Wherever he went, the striking white haired and bearded figure drew great crowds, although his general health was now failing. On 9 May 1912, he made his momentous 'I'll fight' speech to seven thousand Salvationists in London's Royal Albert Hall. This was his last public appearance. He told his audience that he was 'going into dry dock for repairs.' An unsuccessful cataract operation was performed on his left eye. The General was now completely

Above: William Booth toured the Holy Land in 1905

Above: Between 1904-1911, William Booth completed no less than seven Motor Campaigns, which took him the length and breadth of the country. Several cars were used for the motor tours in different years. The car above (a Daracq) was often described simply as 'the big white car with red wheels'

blind. 'Bramwell', he said, as he broke the news to his son, 'I have done what I could for God and the people with my eyes. Now I shall see what I can do for God and the people without my eyes.'

There was very little time left for William to fulfil his words. His health began to deteriorate rapidly, and on 20 August 1912, the eighty-three year-old General of the Salvation Army received his own promotion to glory. On 21 August, the window of the International Headquarters in Queen Victoria Street bore the simple message: 'The General has laid down his sword.' In sixty years of ministry William had travelled five million miles, preached sixty thousand sermons, and inspired sixteen thousand officers to serve the cause in fifty-eight countries.

William's body lay in state in the Congress Hall, Clapton, where sixty-five thousand grief stricken people filed past the coffin to pay their respects to the man whom the Mayor of South Shields had described as 'The Archbishop of the World'. The memorial service reflected the breadth of social scale that William had bridged in his lifetime. On Tuesday 27 August 1912, thirty-five thousand people packed the Olympia Exhibition Hall, where twenty-two years earlier William had said farewell to his beloved Catherine. It is claimed that Queen Mary arrived unannounced and took her seat alongside a woman who confessed that she had once been a prostitute, but had been saved by the work of The Salvation Army. Salvation Army officers from all over the world sat with recent converts, rescued from the gutters of London.

The Salvation Army's high command requested that their founder be buried in Westminster Abbey, but this was refused. The doors that were swung open to receive the body of Charles Darwin were firmly shut on William Booth!

It was more fitting that William's body should be laid to rest alongside Catherine in Abney Park Cemetery. On Thursday 29 August, accompanied by the music of forty bands, seven thousand Salvationists marched behind the cortege, as the procession made the five-mile journey from the Victoria Embankment to Stoke Newington. Immense crowds turned out to pay tribute. Businesses were closed as the procession passed through the City, where the Lord Mayor of London stood in silent tribute. At the graveside, amid floral tributes from the King and Queen, and many other heads of state, the Army's new General, Bramwell

Above: In June 1904, William Booth was invited to Buckingham Palace to meet King Edward VII. William was astonished when the King asked him for his autograph!

Facing page: Westminster Abbey: in the Chapel of St George, a commemorative plaque hangs to the memory of General Booth

Booth, addressed the crowd: 'If you were to ask me, I think I could say that the happiest man I ever knew was the General. . . I rode the other morning on a ministering journey with Commissioner Sturgess up a little lane in Limehouse, in the East End of London, and oh, how my mind turned back to forty years ago, and to a fishmonger's shop there! The fishmonger was friendly to us, and used to take out the windows of his shop for us on Sunday mornings. I have heard the General from behind that fish counter pouring out his soul on the people.' Bramwell concluded, 'I loved him, and you loved him, and he was our leader. He led us and we are going to follow him.'

And follow him they did. Today, in this corner of Abney Park Cemetery, united in death, are the graves of Bramwell Booth, Elijah Cadman, George Scott Railton and others. Meanwhile, those who

WILLIAM BOOTH
FOUNDER AND
FIRST GENERAL
OF
THE
SALVATION
ARMY
1829 - 1912

Above: Opened in 1886, the Grand Hall, Olympia was the setting for the funeral service of William Booth in 1912
Below: The funeral procession reaches Mansion House in London

continue to follow still bring 'soup, soap and salvation', to the poor on every continent of the world.

What was it that enabled William Booth to achieve so much for God and mankind? The two children who had remained in active service for the Salvation Army gave the answer. Bramwell recalled that William had once told him of the time when he had knelt at the table in Broad Street Methodist Chapel, Nottingham and vowed, 'that God would have all there is of William Booth.' Later, General Evangeline added, 'That really wasn't his secret—his secret was that he never took it back!'

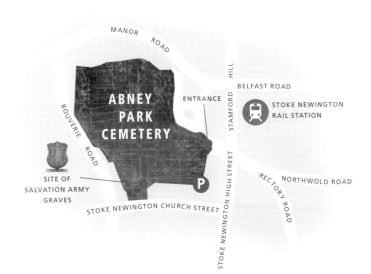

The Congestion Charge and difficulty with parking make it advisable to use public transport when travelling in Central London.

Abney Park Cemetery

William Booth was 'promoted to glory' on 20 August 1912. He was buried in Abney Park Cemetery, Stoke Newington on 29 August 1912. Also buried here are: Catherine Booth, William Bramwell Booth, Miriam Booth, Marian Billups Booth, George Scott Railton, Elijah Cadman, and other Salvation Army pioneers.

Above: *The Grave of William and Catherine Booth at Abney Park Cemetery*

At the centre of the cemetery is a statue of the hymn writer, Isaac Watts. It is to commemorate his stay at Abney House, on whose grounds the cemetery stands. Watts is buried in Bunhill Fields, opposite Wesley's House and Chapel in London.

The cemetery is situated in Stoke Newington, London, N16. The main entrance is at the junction

of Stoke Newington High Street, Northwold Road, and Stamford Hill.

By car: Parking at the Cemetery or in Church Street. There is an entrance to the cemetery opposite Booth's grave.

By public transport: Rail: Stoke Newington (from Liverpool Street). On leaving the station, turn left and cross the main road at the first pedestrian crossing. Continue in the same direction. The entrance to the cemetery is on the right. Bus service: 73 from Oxford Circus; 76 from Waterloo Station; 149 from London Bridge Station; 67 from Wood Green; 106 from Finsbury Park.

On entering the cemetery, bear left onto a gravel path (Abney Park is also a nature reserve and is overgrown in places). Continue until you come to an open area, where, on the right is the grave of William Booth.

Top: *Immense crowds turned out to pay tribute as William Booth's funeral cortege passed through the City on its way to Abney Park Cemetery*

Below: *The statue in memory of the hymn writer Isaac Watts who died in 1745 at Abney House, in the grounds of which the cemetery stands. Watts is buried in Bunhill Fields, London*

Olympia Exhibition Centre

Hammersmith Road, London, W14 8U8
☎ 020 7385 1200

The Grand Hall, opened on Boxing Day 1886, was the venue for both Catherine and William Booth's funeral services. It was expanded in 1923 and again in 1929. The

The Royal Albert Hall

present building was completed in 1959. Nearby are the Natural History, Science and Victoria and Albert Museums. The V&A contains a very good model of the Crystal Palace as it was in William Booth's day.

By car: parking information ☎ 0800 056 8444

By public transport: Rail—Kensington Olympia. Underground—Kensington Olympia (District line from Earl's Court). Bus service—9, 27, 10, 49, 28, 391 London transport information ☎ 020 7222 1234.

Westminster Abbey

Situated next to Parliament Square, opposite the Houses of Parliament.
☎ 020 7222 7110 (information desk). Email: info@westminster-

abbey.org

Open to visitors Monday—Friday 0900—1645 hrs (last admission 1545 hrs). Conducted tours are available. There is an admission charge. There is no tourist visiting on Sundays, but visitors are welcome to the services of worship (no admission charge). There are facilities for the disabled (please check with information desk).

Although William Booth was refused burial here, a memorial plaque was unveiled in the Chapel of St George in 1965. Many other figures from British history are buried and remembered here.

By car: parking in the area is very difficult.

By public transport: Underground—St James' Park (District and Circle lines) and Westminster (Jubilee, District and Circle lines). Bus services—3, 11, 12, 24, 53, 77A, 88, 159, 211

The Royal Albert Hall

Kensington Gore, London, SW7 2AP
☎ 020 7589 8212 (bookings) and 020 7589 3853 (for information for disabled visitors)
Officially opened by Queen Victoria in 1871, this is where William Booth gave his last public address on 9 May 1912. The Hall is used for various public events, including the famous Promenade Concerts from July—September each year. Tours of the Hall are conducted but check availability first.

By car: a public car park is situated in Prince Consort Road. There is limited parking at the Hall and that must be booked first.

By public transport: Underground—South Kensington (District, Circle and Piccadilly lines) half mile walk to Hall. Bus services—9, 10, 52.

BELFAST

NOTTINGHAM

EDINBURGH

TYNESIDE

SPALDING

BELFAST

DUBLIN

CARDIFF

LONDON

DUBLIN

CORNWALL

CORNWALL

WORTHING

UNITED KINGDOM AND EIRE

Useful information

You may be a very experienced traveller who has learned all the tips to make for a pleasant day of touring. The following notes are for those who are new to visiting places of interest and especially for overseas visitors; a little information about your host country will make you feel more at home and less of a stranger. Travelling around in the UK is easy if a few things are remembered.

1 What do you wear?
Wear comfortable clothes and shoes. Travelling on public transport can be hot and dirty; so it is better to dress comfortably than smartly. Wear thin layers (relevant to the season) topped with a light waterproof coat that can protect from wind as well as rain. It is easier to carry two or more thinner garments than a heavy coat and jumper if the weather changes from cold to fine. Remember that the only reliable thing about the British weather is that it is unreliable!

2 Take great care with personal belongings.
Keep wallets and purses out of sight, on your person, as bags can easily be snatched. Cameras and other personal items should be kept secure at all times. A rucksack may be good for your back, but be careful on crowded public transport or in bustling city streets, it can be opened and items removed without your knowledge. Never put a bag down and walk off, it will probably have disappeared when you return—it may have been stolen or possibly blown up as a suspected bomb! All this is especially important in our cities and towns, but don't assume that your property is more secure just because you are in the heart of rural Britain. Being aware of possible problems will enable you to enjoy your sightseeing. Normally when precautions are taken an incident will not arise. And rest easy—Britain is still one of the safest countries in the world to travel around in, and the evidence of this is that most police do not carry guns.

3 For overseas visitors.
Do not carry your passport with you, unless you plan to change money.

Most hotels have a safe where you can store valuable items. If you think you may need your passport for identification often a photocopy will do. In fact it is a good idea to take a photocopy of the relevant pages of your passport and carry this with you always, separate from the original passport. If the original is lost then it will be easier for your embassy to issue a temporary document from the information on the photocopy.

4 Obtain a map of public transport in the
area you are travelling. Basic maps are free from tourist information kiosks; bus and railway maps are available from bus garages (depots/terminus) and major railway stations. If a particular site mentioned in this book is on the mainline

railway network then the station is referred to and instructions of the best way to get to it are given.

5 Always respect the places you visit.

Take note of 'No Entry' and 'Private' signs. A private dwelling may once have had a connection with the subject of this book, but the present residents may consider it an intrusion if you disturb them. We have tried to indicate where access is or is not permitted. Usually there will be an indication at the property if it is open for public viewing.

6 Photography. Respect any 'No Photographs permitted' signs, and if a fee is requested to take photographs then it must be paid. In some museums and historic buildings you may take photographs, but you are not permitted to use a tripod since this can be very annoying to other visitors. Please bear this in mind when deciding on the speed of film you buy. The general rule should be never to use a camera in museums and historic buildings without enquiring first. A polite enquiry can save hassle. Take

enough film for the day. You are well advised not to buy film from a street vendor, however cheap they may appear; old or poor quality film can ruin your valuable memories. Always buy in a reputable shop, and get a receipt in case the film is faulty. Look for the 'three for the price of two' offers during the peak season.

7 In a museum, exhibition or church, do not touch anything that you are not permitted to

handle. Not only can an object be damaged, but also in certain circumstances prosecution may result because of your action, however unintended it may have been.

8 Respect graves. In a cemetery, church or churchyard, please be careful where you tread, especially if a service is taking place. A good rule of thumb is to consider how you would feel if someone came and disturbed the resting-place of your loved ones. You may want to stand on a tomb or

grave to get a good photograph, but remember that this could cause offence. Walk around a church or graveyard without raising your voice; someone may be sitting quietly by the grave of their loved one.

9 When walking in the countryside, please respect the country code. Leave gates as you found them—whether open or closed. Keep to the paths, or walk around the edge of fields. Please do not drop litter—farm animals are not very smart and will chew on your discarded plastic bags and take-away dishes, often with tragic results. Animals should be left in peace, and if you have a dog with you, make sure that it does not worry any livestock. Be very careful not to start a fire, especially in hot dry weather.

10 Litter. Please be careful with the disposal of all litter. In many cities it will not be easy to find litter bins due to terrorist activities. Therefore you may have to take your rubbish back home with you. Chewing Gum. If you use

gum please be careful in the disposal of it after use, some places are considering bringing in heavy fines to deter thoughtless discarding of it; and reference libraries will ask you to remove it from your mouth if they see you chewing!

11 You will probably find it useful to put together a tourist pack.
We suggest the following: a notebook, a pen or pencil, a small torch with batteries that work and a small medical kit. These things will not take up a lot of room but may be useful to you at some stage.

12 Eating out.
For most trips you may prefer to prepare a packed lunch. This can save time looking around for suitable food outlets. Remember that city eating places can be expensive. If a hot meal is required there are many different types of food outlets to suit all tastes and styles. Many Garden Centres have excellent cafeterias or restaurants and are usually good value for money. These are normally open for food

between 10.00am and 4.00pm. Good rural public houses (pubs) can also provide quality service.

13 Disabled visitors.
All public buildings in the UK are under a legal requirement to be wheelchair accessible; those in charge of such places are usually very helpful, but in old buildings full access is not always possible. We have indicated where access may be difficult or where there may be particular problems, or special facilities, for the disabled, visually impaired or the hard of hearing. Please let us know if you discover things that have deteriorated—or improved.

14 Public conveniences (restrooms).
In cities these are usually open until about 6pm. Most major stores, large petrol stations and

every restaurant or café will have conveniences. As a last resort if it is late or you are in a small village, there is usually one in a public house. Some landlords will not be happy for you to just walk in to use the convenience, if in doubt buy a snack (crisps or nuts etc.) this usually pacifies them. Always carry tissues (Kleenex) with you, as some public conveniences will not have any toilet tissue; better to be safe than sorry.

15 Especially for London.
A London combined network map (bus, underground (tube) and overland railway) is available from bus garages, underground

stations, overland railway stations and also many newsagents who display the London transport sign. Travel to all London sites will be referred to from one of the main London termini. If you are staying on the outskirts of London or travelling in for the day from another location, note beforehand where you need to be and how long it will take you to get there, a little planning can save wasted time (see page 128). The best time to travel around London on a weekday is after 9.30am. You can save a lot of money if your train leaves after this time, and you avoid the rush hour. The transport companies have divided London into zones, and the number of zones visited will determine the cost of the ticket. The best ticket to buy is a Travel card (you can get daily, weekly or monthly cards). Travel cards will enable the user to go by overland train, tube and bus all on the same ticket. Make sure that you buy the right ticket for the places to be visited; just ask the clerk in the ticket office, they will tell you the best ticket for your needs.

Refreshments in London are many and various. It would be best to have a packed lunch but if you prefer hot food, please take note of the following: always check that the food and drink prices are listed before you place an order; this way you will not end up paying unnecessarily high prices. If it appears that you are a foreigner, or from out of town it is not unknown for extras to suddenly appear on a bill (check). Always query any discrepancies before payment is made. Drinks and food from roadside vendors in the cities will be more expensive.

Unless you have a good budget, the best places for light refreshments are fast food restaurants, especially if you just want a hot drink. Another possibility worth investigating is any café that builders are using! They may not be the most luxurious surroundings, but the workers normally know where to find good wholesome food, that is served quickly and hot—and at a reasonable price. You will also gain an interesting insight into London life!

Finally—well, nearly!

These basic guidelines are not meant to hinder but enhance your enjoyment as you travel around.
If on your travels you come across other sights or places of related interest not mentioned in this book, would you kindly let the publisher know, and any future edition may be able to include this information for the enjoyment of other travellers.

Enjoy your journey!

Useful Telephone Numbers

In an emergency call ☎ **999** and ask for Fire, Police or Ambulance.
Remember to tell the operator, **Where the trouble is, What the trouble is, Where you are.** Also give the number of the phone you are using. Never make a false call, you could risk the lives of others that really need help and
it is against the law. You can also be traced immediately to the phone where the call came from.

If you need help in making a call that is Local or National, call free on ☎ **100**. If help is required in making an International call, call free on ☎ **155**.

If you require help in finding a number or code call Directory Enquiries.

Travelodge reservations: ☎ 08700 850 950. www.travelodge.co.uk

Travel Inn reservations: ☎ 0870 242 8000.

Tourist Information Centres: www.mistral.co.uk/hammerwood/uk.htm

National Rail enquiries: ☎ 0845 7 48 49 50. Or for the hard of hearing, 0845 60 50 600. www.rail.co.uk

London Transport: ☎ 020 7222 1234 www.londontransport.co.uk/ London Transport www.londontransport.co.uk/

Transport for London: www.transportforlondon.gov.uk

BIBLIOGRAPHY

Barnes, Cyril, *Booth's England,* Egon Publishers, 2000

Barnes, Cyril, *With Booth in London,* Salvation Army, 1989

Begbie, Harold, *Life of William Booth* (2 Vols.), Macmillan, 1920 (Out of print)

Collier, Richard, *The General Next to God,* Collins, 1965

Hattersley, Roy, *Blood and Fire,* Abacus, 1999

Hosier, Helen K., *William and Catherine Booth,* Barbour, 1999

The Author

Jim Winter has been an evangelical Pastor in England for over twenty years and has preached and lectured in the UK and overseas. He holds a PhD in Pastoral Psychotherapy. He is the author of *Depression: a rescue plan* published by Day One. After a long period of ministry in London's inner city, he now lives and works in West Sussex. He is married to Marie and they have two sons.

ALSO IN THIS SERIES

TRAVEL WITH CH SPURGEON

Clive Anderson

ISBN.1 903087 11 2

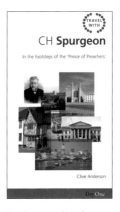

Few have combined so many gifts and achievements in such a short lifetime as Charles Haddon Spurgeon. During his forty-one years as a Christian pastor and preacher, Spurgeon published one hundred and fifty books, while preaching regularly to congregations of 6,000, in addition to launching almost seventy charitable causes, many of which still exist today. His impact was so great, that over a century after his death he is still read by millions on every continent.

Travel with Spurgeon will enable you to follow his life and retrace his journey—from a teenage country pastor to the

largest congregation in the capital city of the British Empire—during the heyday of Victorian preaching.

Other titles include:

Travel with John Bunyan
Travel with John Knox

1829
*10 April Born
Sneinton
Nottingham*

1844
*Converted at
Broad Street
Chapel
Nottingham*

1849
*Arrives in
London for the
first time*

1851
*Meets Catherine
Mumford*

1852
*Begins a
preaching
ministry in
Spalding*

1865
*Start of the
'Christian
Mission' London*

1878
*'Christian
Mission' became
the 'Salvation
Army'*

1890
*4 October
Catherine dies*

1912
*20 August
'Promoted to
Glory'*

Below: *William Booth's funeral procession reaches the gates of Abney Park Cemetery, Stoke Newington (29 August 1912)*

1829	Born at 12 Notintone Place, Sneinton, Nottingham (10 April)
1842	Father dies and William became a pawnbroker
1844	Converted at Broad Street Wesleyan Chapel, Nottingham
1849	Arrives in London for the first time
1851	Meets Catherine Mumford
1852	Financed by Edward Harris Rabbits. Christian ministry in Spalding, Lincolnshire (resigned in 1854)
1854	Accepted into membership of New Connexional Methodist Church as a probationary minister
1855	Marries Catherine at Stockwell Green Congregational Church (16 June)
	Works in York, Dewsbury, Leeds, Halifax, Midlands (1855–57)
1856	William Bramwell born (8 March)
1857	Ballington born (29 July)
	Booth appointed to New Connexional settled ministry
1858	Daughter Catherine born (18 September)
	Booth ordained (27 May)
1859	Catherine publishes tract on Female Ministry
	Booth works in Tyneside
1860	Emma born (8 January)
1861	Returns to London; Resigns from New Connexion to become itinerant evangelist
	Works in Cornwall
1862	Herbert born (26 August)
	Booth works in Cardiff
1864	Marian born (4 May)
1865	Start of the 'Christian Mission' London
1865	Evangeline Cory born (25 December)
1878	'Christian Mission' becomes the 'Salvation Army'
1890	Catherine dies (4 October)
	Publication of *In Darkest England and the Way Out*
1891	Industrial and Farm Colony inaugurated in Hadleigh, Essex
1896	First Salvation Army Exhibition, Agricultural Hall, London
1904	Received by Edward VII
1905	Prays before US Senate
	Campaigns in Holy Land, Australia and New Zealand
	Receives freedom of London and Nottingham
1907	Receives honorary degree at Oxford (Doctor of Civil Law) (26 June)
	Received by kings of Denmark and Norway, Queen of Sweden and Emperor of Japan
1912	Last public address (9 May)
	Death (20 August) Funeral at Abney Park Cemetery (29 August)

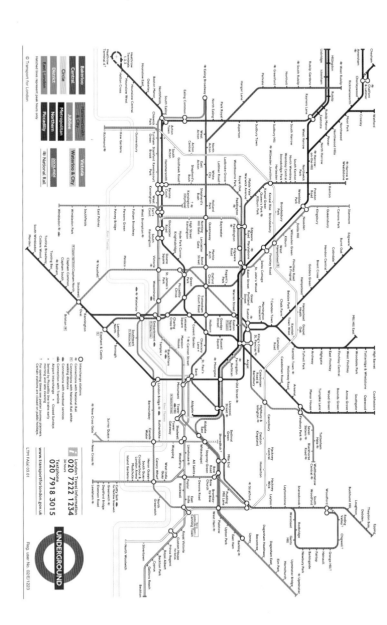